Contemporary Netsuke

1 (*Frontispiece*). INRO, OJIME, AND NETSUKE. Inro by Koma Yasu-masa (also known as Koma Ankyo; d. 1715). Netsuke and ojime unsigned, *c.* 18th century. Courtesy of Virginia Atchley. (En-largement: 1.7 times)

MIRIAM KINSEY

Contemporary 根附 Netsuke

with a Foreword by Hans Conried

Photographs by Tomo-o Ogita
and Tsune Sugimura

Sketches by Adelheid Roth Roscher

CHARLES E. TUTTLE COMPANY

Rutland · Vermont : Tokyo · Japan

REPRESENTATIVES

For Continental Europe:
BOXERBOOKS, INC., *Zurich*
For the British Isles:
PRENTICE-HALL INTERNATIONAL, Inc., *London*
For Australasia:
BOOK WISE (AUSTRALIA) PTY. LTD.
104-108 Sussex Street, Sydney

Published by the Charles E. Tuttle Company, Inc.
of Rutland, Vermont & Tokyo, Japan
with editorial offices at
Suido 1-chome, 2-6, Bunkyo-ku, Tokyo

Copyright in Japan, 1977
by Charles E. Tuttle Co., Inc.

Library of Congress Catalog Card No. 77-072596
International Standard Book No. 0-8048 1159-8

Book design, typography, and layout
by F. Sakade and H. Doki

First printing, 1977
Second printing, 1983

PRINTED IN JAPAN

To my husband Bob

and

To all who are keeping

the art of netsuke carving alive

Table of Contents

List of Illustrations

Foreword

by HANS CONRIED

THESE LATE years have witnessed an amazing proliferation of books and articles on netsuke. The treasure first mined by Brockhaus and Weber has been ably refined and mounted by many latter-day scholar-collectors and enhanced by the miracles of modern photographic reproduction, so that we now have answers to almost all our questions about the good old masters and the good old works that have fascinated collectors for a century. One might well believe that, save for reports of occasional new discoveries, little remains to be said. Or so it seemed until the arduous spadework of Mrs. Kinsey revealed that wonders have not ceased and that the netsuke tradition is alive and flourishing in our own time.

"Netsuke-itis" is now a common affliction, an intense acquisitive urge that subsides, normally, only with the onset of severe financial insufficiency. Two general categories of the disease emerge: a craving for the old and a craving for the new. Despite the virulent nature of the disorder, it would now seem that sufferers from both varieties can safely share the same ward, and sometimes even the same bed.

This patient can diagnose his own malady as the kind most prevalent thirty years ago. This was, understandably, a predilection for the "honto" or "true" netsuke, with its aura of samurai times, the signs of wear from usage, the "good color" (if ivory), and the contained form that made it practical. Pieces of this type were readily available, at modest prices, to the collector who had an early start in the quest. True, new netsuke were offered for sale occasionally—the specimens from the So school, for example, which were always of a very high order, even if sometimes "too fussy." But these pieces we were inclined to think unworthy of our attention. Perhaps more to the point, they were considerably dearer than the far more numerous old netsuke whose makers were no longer concerned with the price of rice. This fact, for me at least, may have added an acidity to grapes that hung high.

But times change, and opinions, opportunities, and tastes change with them. Today the demand from collectors and speculative dealers far exceeds the supply of available netsuke, old or new, good or bad. And a whole new generation of young Japanese carvers has been inspired to engage in a craft that not many years ago seemed to be dead or dying. They carve as well as many of their forebears, and their work is more and more in demand.

Here, then, is the book collectors have been waiting for: a thorough compilation of those craftsmen and artists of our own time who, although frankly serving collector rather than wearer, maintain so high a standard of dedicated skill that their work can be judged with that of the old masters.

Mrs. Kinsey, with enterprise, energy, and effort, and, I am sure, with Mr. Kinsey's generous help, has placed the lives and works of these contemporary *netsuke-shi* within reach of our grateful hands.

Acknowledgments

NUMEROUS people and circumstances, both related and unrelated, plus an understanding husband who shares my enthusiastic addiction to netsuke collecting, have contributed to this study of contemporary netsuke carvers and their work.

Because of the language and distance barriers, the research involved would have been impossible without the competent, dedicated, and loving help of our friend Michiko Matsumoto, who lived with us in California for more than a year while she was studying at U.C.L.A. Michi handled my relations with all of the officers and members of the Japan Ivory Sculptors Association, as well as with dealers and other sources of information. Since the carvers speak no English, she acted as interpreter during all visits with them and translated their written answers to questions. She coordinated picture-taking sessions for Mr. Sugimura and followed through on countless points that had to be checked or expanded. She secured signatures and biographical material from carvers and researched innumerable bits of minutiae that are imperceptible but necessary in a book of this nature. In short, without Michi it would have been virtually impossible for me to complete this book.

The Japan Ivory Sculptors Association, through its officers, its members, and particularly the committee appointed to help me, has been of inestimable assistance. Mr. Toshitake Nakamura, secretary, has spent countless hours getting questionnaires to member carvers, securing proper signatures, and checking and rechecking innumerable details.

I am deeply indebted to a number of dealers, not only for their help in building our collection of contemporary netsuke but also for their assistance in contacting carvers and providing personal information about them: to Mr. Hirokazu Nakayama, of Tokyo, from whom we bought our first netsuke, and subsequently many more, and to his father in Kyoto, now deceased; to

19

Mr. Herman Krupp, an importer in Seattle, whose love and knowledge of netsuke was an inspiration to us during the beginning years of our collecting; to Mr. Kohachiro Yokoyama, of Kyoto, who was responsible for our meeting Keiun and Yukimasa; to Mr. Seiichiro Sunamoto, of Tokyo, and his assistant Mrs. Hashimoto, who arranged our first meeting with Hodo, with Shodo, and with Ryushi; to Mr. Tadao Miyakoshi, through whom we first met Koyu; to Mr. S. Kaneko, of Yokohama, whose association with several of the leading carvers spans several decades; to Mr. Y. Watanabe, of Yokohama and Tokyo, who provided much information about Yoshiyuki, Gaho, and other carvers; to Mrs. N. T. Wakayama of the Asahi Art Co., Tokyo; to Mr. K. Kitagawa; to Mr. Yoshiaki Ohno, of Tokyo; and to Mr. T. Inoue, of Miyanoshita. To Mr. Raymond Bushell, of Tokyo, I am indebted for information about Masatoshi and the picture of him on page 184.

Our first introduction to a carver was arranged by Mr. Nakayama, through Mr. Shigeo Tsujita, who acted as agent for several first-rank carvers. We were taken by him to the home of Ichiro Inada, who became a close personal friend. Mr. Tsujita subsequently arranged for us to meet Yoko and Shogetsu. We were saddened in the fall of 1971 to learn of the death of Mr. Tsujita, to whom we are greatly indebted. We are also indebted to Mr. Tsujita's son for his helpful information in several areas.

Other Japanese friends who have been most generous with their help, particularly in the translating area, include Mr. Kevin Kuniyoshi, of Los Angeles, and Mr. Yoshihiro Saito, of Washington, D.C.

A number of our netsuke-collecting friends have graciously loaned some of their treasures for inclusion in this book: Virginia Atchley, Frontispiece and Figs. 22 and 108; Ann Meselsen, Fig. 116; Hans Conried, Figs. 60, 61, and 62. Mr. Bernard Hurtig kindly loaned us two netsuke: Bumbuku Chagama and Urashima Taro, which served as models for sketches on pages 86 and 90.

A Los Angeles friend, Janet Gross, formerly with *Time* and *Life*, was most helpful in making suggestions and corrections in my manuscript.

I have been very fortunate in having two photographers whose exceptional talents have been equaled by their great enthusiasm and intelligent interest in the contemporary carvers and their work: Mr. Tsune Sugimura of Tokyo, Japan's foremost folk-craft photographer and head of one of Japan's most active photography studios, a member of the Japan Society of Photographers, a lecturer at Tokyo's Tama University of the Arts, and an author whose fine work is familiar to Westerners in *The Enduring Crafts of Japan;* and Mr. Tomo-o Ogita, of Los Angeles, a leading Oriental authority and educator, the director of the Japan Ukiyo-e Society of Los Angeles, and owner of Asia Art Associates.

I am also grateful to George Lazarnick for permission to use his photographs of the signatures of Shoko (page 230) and Sosui (page 231).

Mrs. Adelheid Roth Roscher, my good friend and neighbor, who did the pen-and-ink sketches throughout the book, studied at the Academy of Fine Arts in Vienna and in Munich, where she obtained her master's degree in art education. She did postgraduate work with Emil Preetorius, President of the Munich Academy and Dean of the Department of Illustration and Scenic Design. After freelancing, she taught at the Luisengymnasium, Bavaria's oldest school for women. At present, she does medical exhibits and contributes illustrations to publications for the International College of Surgeons, of which her husband, Arno A. Roscher, M.D., is an active member. She had never seen a netsuke before starting her sketches. She is now an avid netsuke collector.

Many netsuke collectors deserve my thanks for sharing with me their beautiful collections and their vast knowledge of the world of netsuke. I am also indebted to a number of carvers for lineage information and for human-interest stories about other carvers, who are reluctant to talk about themselves. I have gratefully relied on Ichiro, Shofu, Kangyoku, Meigyokusai, and other carvers for help in compiling the chapter on techniques.

Finally, the guiding and prodding spirit in this project has been my husband, Bob. His love of Japan is so great that he welcomed the excuse of research on my book to turn our vacation steps in that direction. He has been a severe but always helpful critic. He has been an understanding husband when housework has taken second place to work on the book. Writing such a book has involved much more effort and time than I visualized at the outset. I must confess the time element was extended by the affectionate interference of our little dachshund, Suki-san, who was always at my feet as I worked. But it has been a gratifying experience because of the enthusiastic cooperation of everyone concerned, the grateful anticipation of the carvers, and most of all, the loving interest and help from my husband. And it has been fun!

Photographers' Notes

SEVERAL years ago when Mrs. Miriam Kinsey contacted me and requested that I do some photographic work for a book she was compiling on contemporary Japanese netsuke, my countenance must have divulged my inner reaction. I felt that anyone so involved with "new" netsuke must be a "naive foreigner," unaware of the beauty of traditional Japanese arts and of "old" netsuke carvings. While watching Mrs. Kinsey speak, I immediately recognized the deep attachment she had for the little netsuke objects she held in her hands. To her they were like little living objects. I also noticed that she had respect and admiration for the contemporary ivory and wood carvers, since she spoke about them as dear friends. Needless to say, I accepted the photographic task because I felt a kindred spirit with Mrs. Kinsey and also because I was delighted to face the creative and technical challenge the project offered me.

For the past thirty years, I have been "a fellow crazy about Oriental bowls, pots, and paintings" and my life has revolved around them. During the past ten years, thanks to Mrs. Kinsey, I have become acquainted with the names of most of the outstanding contemporary netsuke carvers of Japan, and I have become truly familiar, through visual and tactile experiences, with the "new" netsuke. And, surprisingly, I have found a great many of them truly outstanding as honest expressions of creativity on the part of the skilled artist-craftsmen. In many cases, I must admit that from the skill and artistic integrity of some of the living carvers have come "new" netsuke masterpieces just as great as, or even greater than, the masterpieces of the past.

Before pointing my large 4-by-5 camera lens and the lights toward each netsuke, I have made it a habit to hold the gentle object in my hands and to "communicate" with it through my fingertips, with my eyes, and even with words. Would you be surprised if I told you that each netsuke has taken the trouble to relate something to me? Some messages have come through in soft

22

whispers while others were loud bellows. I have learned, not only through the netsuke but also through handling other art objects, that each item is a crystallized formation of the love that possessed its creator. Without this deep devotion to one's art or craft and to the objects produced, how can one expect these little items to survive the gigantic waves of changes of the times?

Each object has given me a challenge to show it in its most advantageous pose and to make certain that I can still help maintain the "life spirit" of the netsuke. If I have succeeded in capturing the spirit and form of the netsuke even to a small degree, I must first credit the netsuke carvers for their originality and Mrs. Kinsey for her patience, kindness, and trust.

TOMO-O OGITA

Los Angeles, California

*   *   *

IN YEARS past, many craftsmen in Japan were called "masters" (*meijin*). However, there are only a few people of this type left today—people whose lives revolve around one skill or one craft, like the metalsmith who can produce oxidized silver. In some cases, there may be only one person, or perhaps no one, left in all of Japan to carry on a specific traditional craft.

The contemporary artists of Japan who are shown in the pages of this book are still quietly working in the authentic tradition of their craft. These netsuke carvers are people who have their art truly in their hands and are manifesting the skills of the traditional *meijin*.

It is my thought that the hands of the craftsmen or the netsuke carvers are precious creative instruments. With their skilled hands, the raw wood or ivory is soon transformed into something new. We are told that the value of the item starts from that point.

A work created in earlier years is passed on to someone in the next generation. Based on the way of life of that time, as well as the thoughts given to the work over a long period of time, changes will be reflected in the color and form of the work. Tradition changes with the life and times of the people and readily shows how strongly the beauty of the object influences our life and livelihood.

The hands that have worked to make things eventually discover "creativity," and the created objects, each with special characteristics, bring joy to our senses. There in front of our eyes we do not view a manufactured item but an object made by the hands of man. Machines cannot produce such work. An object made by the skilled hands of an artist gives aesthetic joy to the beholder and also imparts the realization that one is gazing upon a "true thing."

Fortunately, there are still about twenty first-rank netsuke carvers in the Tokyo area and several in the Kyoto region. By casting light upon these quiet, talented, and dedicated artists, it will be possible to have a larger audience that truly understands the meaning and value of "things made by hand."

TSUNE SUGIMURA

Tokyo, Japan

Introduction

HAVE YOU ever held a netsuke in your hand? It is an experience that may well lead you down enchanting, fun-filled trails.

Perhaps you will first explore the history of netsuke—their origin, their transition from purely functional pendants or toggles to an art form. You will find that the flowering of this art of miniature sculpture paralleled the longest peaceful period in Japanese history (Edo, 1603–1868). During this time, Japan had very little intercourse with the rest of the world. Because of the lack of foreign influence, the art of netsuke carving, like the art of woodblock printing, which also flourished during this period, represents an expression of pure Japanese creativeness, beauty, and artistic skill.

If the subject matter of the first two or three netsuke you acquire is based on legends or folklore, and you start down that trail, you will be off on a never ending adventure. You will be introduced to the life and customs, the history, and the religion of the Japanese people of that period through an art form captivating in its whimsy and incredible in its beauty.

A number of excellent books have been written during the past six or seven decades on the subject of netsuke (see Bibliography). These books have included brief biographies of the carvers and their signatures; photographs of representative netsuke; and information on materials, carving techniques, and subject matter of netsuke produced during the seventeenth, eighteenth, and nineteenth centuries.

Information on twentieth-century carvers and their contribution to the world of netsuke art is extremely limited. The purpose of this book is to explore contemporary netsuke trails; not only for the enlightenment of the collector—both potential and sophisticated—but also to increase recognition of the distinguished work of a comparatively small group of truly superior contemporary netsuke carvers.

In writing this book on the contemporary netsuke scene, I have tried to be as representative and as up-to-date as possible. (More or less arbitrarily, I defined "contemporary" as the period from 1925 to the present.) But changes have occurred since the manuscript was completed: promising carvers have become important ones; new talents have emerged; and, unhappily, distinguished figures have vanished from the landscape. For any lapses or inaccuracies caused by such changes I must ask my readers' indulgence. As with any book on contemporary art, there had to be a cut-off point for current information.

—THE AUTHOR

Note: As this book was nearing publication, we received the very sad news of Ichiro's death on June 22, 1977.

Part One

CHAPTER 1

Background

NETSUKE AND SCULPTURAL ART

With the introduction of Buddhism into Japan in A.D. 552 a whole new world of sculptural art was born. Buddhist images and image carvers came to Japan from China, and the deities of Buddhism provided a wealth of new subject matter for the Japanese artist. Some of the world's finest examples of Buddhist art, the wooden statues of the Nara period (710–94), were produced by Japanese sculptors early in the eighth century. While Chinese canons of art unquestionably had an influence on Japan's sculpture during the Nara period, the true Japanese tradition was never submerged. Subsequent periods were marked by various sculptural innovations, including architectural decorations, masks worn in Noh dramas, sword ornaments and furnishings, the netsuke, and the *ojime*. When netsuke first came into use is not definitely known, although the earliest artistically executed netsuke still in existence date from the end of the sixteenth century.

EARLY PERIOD (c. 1574–1780)

The word *netsuke,* loosely translated, means "root attachment." The absence of pockets in the kimono made netsuke a necessary, functional part of Japanese attire. Their basic origin can be traced to the Muromachi period (1336–1568), when they were presumably worn as toggles attached to a cord tucked under the belt or sash (obi) from which were suspended keys, a water gourd, or various objects known as *koshisage* (things hanging from the waist), or *sagemono* (hanging things). The netsuke of this period were natural forms—a wisteria root, a shell, a small gourd, a bone, a stone, or an uncarved piece of wood (Fig. 2).

The decorated netsuke undoubtedly came into use late in the sixteenth or early in the seventeenth century, when it was the fashion for samurai and the aristocratic classes to carry *inro* (see Frontispiece). The *inro* was a small flat

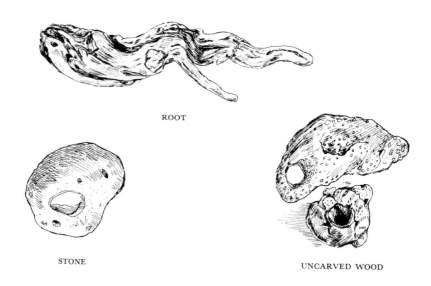

ROOT

STONE

UNCARVED WOOD

2. Natural-form netsuke.

box, usually containing several compartments, and was used to carry medicine or seals. The compartments were neatly fitted, one on top of the other, and were held together by a cord that passed through a bead fastener called an *ojime*. The netsuke was attached to the end of the cord as a toggle to hold the cord under the obi. Money pouches (*kinchaku*) also hung from the obi, held fast with netsuke toggles. These early netsuke were simple in design and generally fashioned in wood, although some in bone, ivory, metal, and lacquer are also attributed to this period.

By the latter part of the seventeenth century the tobacco pouch, held in place at the waist by cord and netsuke, came into use (Fig. 3). During the eighteenth century the practice of pipe smoking became very widespread, with the result that there was an increase in the demand for netsuke. The netsuke became a status symbol, its style and value corresponding to the position and wealth of the wearer.

This booming netsuke market gave occupation to many carvers and lured distinguished artists from other arts and crafts. One of the imperial edicts against the Christians (*c.* 1605) required that a Buddhist image be placed in every home. This led many artists to turn their talents to sculptural art. When the demand for religious images was satisfied, many sculptors then turned their creative skills to netsuke carving. Netsuke of finest quality, in increasing numbers, were coming from the workshops of top-ranking carvers. At the same time, less skillfully wrought netsuke were being produced for those of limited means.

3. Tobacco pouch, pipe (in case), cord, and netsuke.

Prior to this time there were no professional netsuke carvers to pass the art down from generation to generation, as was traditional in the world of Buddhist-image sculptors. Netsuke carving was largely a side industry of various craftsmen, such as maskmakers and dollmakers, metalworkers, lacquerers, image sculptors, and makers of musical instruments. Netsuke carving was also a pastime of dentists, artists, samurai, and men of learning. By the latter part of the eighteenth century, the demand for netsuke became so great that many of the most talented craftsmen turned to netsuke carving as a vocation. Thus began the seventy-year period often referred to as the Golden Age of netsuke art.

THE GOLDEN AGE (c. 1780-1850)

This period reached its zenith during the first three decades of the nineteenth century. The netsuke carvers—both professionals and hobbyists—increased in number. Netsuke in great quantity, some of the finest in quality and most varied in material and design, were produced. The majority of carvers lived in and near large cities—Tokyo (Edo), Kyoto, Osaka, and Nagoya—and because of the great demand, wholesale stores specializing in netsuke were established in these cities. The work of the first-rank carvers could be increasingly recognized by individual style and subject matter, as well as by regional characteristics.

DECLINE (c. 1850-75)

Several factors contributed to the decline of netsuke art during the period immediately preceding and following the Meiji Restoration. With the arrival of Commodore Perry on Japanese shores in 1853 and the reopening of foreign trade, which had been virtually prohibited for over two centuries, Western-style clothing with pockets began to take the place of the kimono, and cigarettes replaced pipes. Ironically, tobacco, which two centuries previously had contributed greatly to the growth of netsuke art through general use of the tobacco pouch, now played a major role in its decline with the introduction of cigarettes.

The restoration of imperial rule brought emphasis on commerce and industry and a diminishing of art appreciation. In 1871 an edict abolished the wearing of swords, the very heart of the samurai tradition. Thus the wearing of *inro* and netsuke by samurai and the upper classes became a custom of the past, and netsuke moved from a traditional place in formal Japanese apparel to the status of collectors' items.

THE BEGINNING OF THE COLLECTING ERA (c. 1875)

Following the arrival of the Americans, foreign trade treaties were signed. Meanwhile, civil war broke out between the emperor's progressive party and the shogun. After a bitter struggle, the Tokugawa shogunate fell, and power was restored to the emperor. The year 1868 marked the beginning of the Meiji era, which lasted for forty-four years.

Ruling aristocrats were dispossessed, deprived of income, and forced to sell their art treasures. Their netsuke, now in disuse, together with those belonging to the samurai and other classes, were sold for incredibly small amounts. From that time on, the story of netsuke becomes the story of netsuke collecting among foreigners. Japanese netsuke wholesalers who had set up shops in the large cities during the heyday of netsuke carving became suppliers for exporters. Netsuke quickly became greatly desirable collectors' items, and both the Japanese countryside and junk shops in the cities were ransacked to fill the ever increasing demand from European and American dealers.

It is ironic that the netsuke, which rarely had been recognized or fully appreciated by the Japanese people, should have been one of the art forms to introduce Japan abroad.

During the latter part of the nineteenth century a few Japanese art exhibits were held in London, and in 1891 the Japan Society was founded and subsequently did a great deal to further interest in Japanese art. Even today, many netsuke collectors from all over the world hold membership in this organization.

Some of the largest early collections, running into the thousands of pieces, were to be found in England. Even earlier, French collections came upon the scene. Although smaller than those in England, they were considered of finer quality. Other important collections appeared in America and Germany. Albert Brockhaus, a German collector, began his collecting in 1877 and became a recognized authority on the subject.

As this first generation of netsuke enthusiasts passed away during the first quarter of the twentieth century, most of their collections were sold on the open market. Very few of their heirs shared the netsuke fever, and, with the exception of a large collection that belonged to Sir A. W. Franks and was willed to the British Museum, few became bequests to the public domain. Thus most of the large collections, representing the cream of Japanese netsuke, were broken up and, largely through auction sales, passed into the hands of the second generation of netsuke collectors. One of the outstanding second-generation collectors was M. T. Hindson, widely recognized as a distinguished netsuke scholar.

Prices still were comparatively low, but the day of concentration of very large collections in the hands of a few collectors was over. Thanks to a number of experts and brilliant authorities like Henri Joly, the circle of knowledgeable collectors was widening. Good netsuke could now be found throughout the world in antique shops such as Yamanaka's in London, a branch of the famous Osaka and Kyoto Yamanaka's. They could also be bought in large department stores like Liberty's in London and the Printemps and Bon Marché stores in Paris, and from smaller dealers such as S. Bing, whose Paris shop was a rendezvous for netsuke scholars.

Immediately after World War II, some very fine antique netsuke owned by Japanese families came on the market in various cities in Japan. Many of them were acquired by Americans in the army of occupation at ridiculously low prices, sometimes for a package of cigarettes. Netsuke thus acquired formed the nucleus of several important collections.

The third generation of collectors is now spread throughout the entire world. Netsuke in limited numbers can be found in stores and shops or purchased from private dealers in almost every country, but the major sales of antique masterpieces still are made at the London auctions, where prices occasionally pass the $10,000 mark for a first-rate netsuke by a famous carver.

A collector of antique netsuke today must have a large bank account and an extensive knowledge of a complex, confusing subject. At the same time he must be content with a modest-sized collection. Occasionally, however, a rare bargain can still be found, and there is more challenge and excitement than ever in the quest for and possession of good netsuke.

And collections of "good netsuke" can and should include works of some outstanding living Japanese netsuke carvers. Their skill can match that of the great carvers of the seventeenth, eighteenth, and nineteenth centuries, and their artistry, originality, and imagination represent a fresh and enchanting approach to the traditional netsuke art form.

THE POST-RESTORATION PERIOD (c. 1875–1925)

The netsuke produced in the period roughly covering the last quarter of the nineteenth century and the first quarter of the twentieth century were generally classified as "modern." As the available supply of antique netsuke in Japan began to dwindle, many carvers who had lost their home market began to produce quick, cheap imitations for export. Because these products were so inferior to the beautiful antique netsuke that had been coming from Japan since the reopening of foreign trade, a distorted image was born and still persists in the minds of many collectors: old netsuke are good, and new netsuke are bad per se.

Actually, however, there were still fine netsuke artist-carvers in Japan, and they continued to carve netsuke and instruct young carvers. Their netsuke sales suffered because of the poor quality of many of the "modern" export netsuke, and many carvers turned to making *okimono* (alcove ornaments), which had begun to find favor with foreigners. Often when an *okimono* was ordered by a foreigner, a netsuke was submitted as a design model. If it was satisfactory, the carver was asked to make an *okimono* ten (or more) times netsuke size. The great carvers went more or less underground during this period, as far as netsuke carving was concerned, but they were definitely keeping the centuries-old art alive.

THE CONTEMPORARY PERIOD (c. 1925-present)

By the 1930s, interest in netsuke collecting was showing new life, particularly throughout the United States. This revival was due largely to the illustrated books on netsuke that were being published in English. Also rising in America was a wealthy leisure class that was becoming interested in art collecting and in world travel, especially to the Orient.

Some good contemporary netsuke began to reach foreign markets and were purchased not only by new collectors but also by some of the collectors of antique netsuke who recognized the beauty and expert craftsmanship of these modern pieces. Mediocre and even poor netsuke were also being exported from Japan—and still are—but the first-rank living carvers were beginning to gain some recognition.

And then came World War II. Carvers either went into military service or worked in factories. Ivory could not be imported, so most of the few netsuke that were being carved in leisure hours were made from wood or old billiard balls. It was close to 1950 before contemporary netsuke were once again reaching American and European dealers.

Today, netsuke by top contemporary carvers are sought by a small group of enthusiastic buyers all over the world, and some collectors are specializing in the work of individual carvers. Perhaps more than in any other Japanese art form, contemporary netsuke remain true to the old tradition in subject matter, material, and craftsmanship. There is, however, an originality and freshness in design that delights collectors, as well as tourists who may buy one or two as symbolic mementos of Japan.

CHAPTER 2

Contemporary Netsuke

EVALUATION

Comparisons may be odious, but they are inevitable when evaluating netsuke. In the following explanation of comparative areas in the quality of contemporary and antique netsuke, it must be understood that, unless otherwise noted, only first-class netsuke are considered. These are all *issaku* netsuke, executed completely by one person—the design, the rough carving, the final work, and any color, stain, or inlay that may be added. The cheaper, mass-produced work is called *bungyo*, or division work, with the rough carving (*arabori*) being done by one person and the final work (*shiage*) by at least one other—all from a design furnished by the "manufacturer," dealer, or agent.

Quality might be defined as "the natural or essential character of something" as well as "degree or grade of excellence." Basically, the evaluation of netsuke involves quality of design and subject matter, material, and workmanship.

DESIGN AND SUBJECT MATTER

Design has been said to be the soul of netsuke, but in the eighteenth century, as the use of netsuke spread to all classes and these small carvings began to be regarded as status symbols, excellence of material and workmanship grew in importance.

The early artist-carver was forced by the functional nature of the netsuke to observe certain restrictions in design. Since it passed between the obi and the hip, the netsuke had to be small and rounded, without sharp edges or jutting points that could catch in the kimono material. Its form must not be damaged by the friction involved in its use. Actually, this rubbing often developed a patina (*aji*) that helps in the authentication of an antique netsuke and adds to its beauty. The netsuke had to be sturdy enough to support the hanging object by the cord passing through it. The cord holes (*himotoshi*) were made on the side to be worn next to the body so as not to detract from the design on the front. Even the early functional netsuke, however, were so designed and carved that they were complete in every detail on all sides and usually could stand with perfect balance when not being worn.

The netsuke being produced today have no functional restrictions in design. A protruding cane, a lacy leaf or flower, or sharp stylized lines are no longer precluded and often lend a charm and freshness to the design. However, the netsuke purist may say, "This is not a netsuke. It is a piece of miniature sculpture. It hasn't the feeling of a netsuke." This is an ongoing argument among collectors. Contemporary netsuke carvers also differ on this point. The majority of them adhere to the old fundamental concept in design. Their netsuke are smooth and rounded and have a "good feeling." Others take advantage of the freedom from functional restrictions and produce what actually is sculpture in miniature, or a diminutive *okimono,* sometimes not even adding the *himotoshi,* long the hallmark of a netsuke.

Subject matter will be discussed at greater length in another chapter. In general, however, today's netsuke, like the antique examples, draw from the natural world of flowers, insects, and animals, as well as the vast reservoir of Japanese folklore, history, literature, religion, theater, customs, and social life. Perhaps because of the taste of Western collectors, many animal subjects are found among contemporary netsuke (Figs. 4–23, 25, 26). The legendary figures in contemporary netsuke tend to be somewhat more representational than the exaggerated versions—"grotesqueries," as they are sometimes called—so often found among antique netsuke.

Occasionally a contemporary netsuke bordering on the abstract can be found. "Stylized" might be a more accurate description of this type, or "netsuke with deformations," to use an expression of one of the contemporary carvers (Figs. 26–28). Stylized or abstract, they remain distinctly Japanese.

Although color on wood goes back to the early netsuke of Shuzan (mid-eighteenth century), extensive use of color on ivory began in the twentieth century with Ichiro, who, like many Japanese craftsmen and artists in various fields, was trained as a painter. The general use of color and stain in the netsuke being produced today adds a decorative and vital touch that accentuates the design and helps to bring the little figures to life.

When viewing representative collections of first-rate antique and contemporary netsuke, a person unfamiliar with netsuke art usually remarks that the contemporary netsuke figures seem happier, more pleasing, and less strained and distorted than most antique figures. Some of the carvers today explain this difference by pointing out that in earlier days the carvers were members of the lowest social class. During the Edo and Meiji periods, they felt unhappy and oppressed, and their struggles were often reflected in their art. Today, there is no class distinction. First-rank carvers are beginning to receive recognition for their work, and life in general for the carver and his family is fuller and happier. And undoubtedly the fact that amateur collectors are usually more attracted to pleasing, beautiful netsuke has also had an influence on the basic design attributes of contemporary netsuke figures.

With a lower standard of living as well as lower living costs, carvers of old found that time was of little value. Often months were spent by a carver in producing a masterpiece. Today, because of economic demands and the pressure of unfilled dealers' orders, there is usually a time limitation on the contemporary carver. He feels that this is compensated for by the opportunity he has to develop his talent through study and through the exchange of ideas and techniques. The carvers of antique netsuke often had their own special techniques or workmanship devices, which were closely guarded secrets. This is no longer true. Today there are few, if any, secrets in the techniques of netsuke carving and coloring.

A greater variety of subjects and materials is to be found in antique netsuke than in the contemporary pieces, largely because there are comparatively few first-rate netsuke being produced today. No area of design has been neglected, however, and a specialized collector can always find his own particular subject preference in contemporary netsuke.

Pages from Hokusai's sketchbooks and others, as well as crumpled and worn sketches done by a teacher or a teacher's teacher, can be found in the workrooms of many contemporary carvers. Bookshelves contain volumes on Japanese history and religion, the Noh and the Kabuki dramas, folklore, and legend. An unspoken commitment seems to exist among living artist-carvers to preserve the netsuke as an art form that unlocks the treasures of the whole gamut of Japanese life and culture.

MATERIALS

When decorative, carved netsuke became accessories of attire early in the seventeenth century, the material generally used was wood: cypress (*hinoki*), which was soft; boxwood (*tsuge*), a very hard wood used for more detailed, intricate carving; and many other varieties, including bamboo, yew, black persimmon, mulberry, tea shrub, cherry, and pine. Some carvers also selected Chinese ebony, camphor, and other imported woods.

Ivory was first used by netsuke carvers during the latter part of the seventeenth century, when the shamisen became a popular musical instrument among all classes. Its plectrum was made of ivory, and after the plectrum material had been taken from the elephant tusk, the remnants were made available to netsuke carvers. The fact that these pieces were three-sided accounts for the somewhat triangular shape of many of the netsuke of that period. The better carvers shunned these remnants from the shamisen factories and used only the finest quality of ivory (*tokata*), preferring Siamese and Annamese tusks. Although elephant ivory was the first choice, netsuke carvers also used boar and hippopotamus tusks as well as those of the narwhal and the walrus, often called marine ivories. A highly prized but very rare type of ivory, reddish orange and yellow in color, was that which came from the protuberance around the huge bill of a tropical bird called the hornbill.

Horn was a frequently used material. Staghorn, which actually was antler rather than horn, was preferred, but netsuke carved from water-buffalo and rhinoceros horn are in existence, although rare.

During the early years when netsuke carving was largely a side industry of craftsmen in other art areas, or a hobby of dilettante carvers, many materials —and combinations of materials—were used: agate, jade, coral, amber, marble, porcelain, various metals (usually combined with wood or ivory in the bun-shaped netsuke called *kagamibuta*), woven reeds, and lacquer. As the demand for netsuke increased and netsuke carving became a vocation for many carvers, the variety of materials decreased, and most of the netsuke produced in the nineteenth century were of wood or ivory.

With the end of the netsuke as a functional part of Japanese attire and its emergence as an export and collector's item, ivory became the popular material for these little art objects. This continued until the World War II years, when luxury materials like ivory were not available. Most of the carvers were then either in military service or working in factories, and the few netsuke carved in their spare time were fashioned in wood.

Today there are not over two or three netsuke artist-carvers who work exclusively in wood, although several who generally carve in ivory make an occasional wood netsuke. It would be safe to say, however, that over eighty percent of contemporary netsuke are ivory. Mother-of-pearl, semiprecious stones, and bits of gold and other metals are sometimes used for inlay and decorative purposes. Stain and color are applied quite extensively and always by the artist himself.

First-rank carvers are always concerned about the quality of their netsuke ivory. Fine-grained, lustrous ivory has a tactile quality sought and enjoyed by collectors. Even in stained or colored netsuke, the crossing, reticulated lines of fine ivory are usually distinguishable.

The greater portion of ivory imported into Japan today comes from the Congo, although much also comes from other African areas—Kenya, Zanzibar, Tanganyika, Uganda, South Africa, Mozambique, Zambia, and Nigeria. Ivory from the Congo is the hardest of African ivory, but ivory from India, Thailand, and Cambodia is still harder. Since India and Thailand are now protecting their elephants, ivory from those countries is sold only locally and is no longer exported. It should also be noted that under the Endangered Species Act of 1973 the United States cooperates with the international community in protecting animals threatened with extinction and that any ivory netsuke shipped to or from Japan must be accompanied by a guarantee that the netsuke is made of ivory from an elephant legally killed in the country of origin, which country must be named in the guarantee. The harder ivory is preferred by most netsuke carvers, but soft ivory can be used for fifteen- or sixteen-inch *okimono*.

Since trade restrictions against Communist China have been relaxed, Chinese ivory carvers are making jewelry and various types of decorative figures for the tourist trade. Recognizing the potential in this business, the Chinese government has begun to import ivory for their carvers. This, among other reasons, has caused a sharp rise in the price of ivory in Japan. In fact, the price more than doubled between 1969 and 1971 and has continued to rise.

There are three companies directly importing ivory to Japan: Miyakoshi, Kitagawa, and Kita. Ivory manufacturers, netsuke agents, or dealers can buy tusks at any time, but when the importers are overstocked, they sell at auction. Normally, ivory auctions take place once or twice a month. Usually, a whole tusk must be purchased, but occasionally some "points" (pointed ends of tusks) appear at auction when the African exporter has sent the poorer parts of tusks to other countries and only the points to Japan.

Tusk points are usually bought for netsuke carving and are 50–70 centimeters (20–28 inches) in length. The fine-grained, hard ivory comes from this part of the tusk, which is solid. At the larger end of the point, a slice can sometimes be cut into three triangular pieces for three netsuke. The middle part of the tusk, also solid, can be used for large figures and an occasional netsuke. The bottom, or large end of the tusk, is hollow and can be used for some types of *okimono* as well as for chopsticks, flowers, or accessories. No part of the tusk is wasted.

Netsuke material must be of high grade, and sometimes there will be no ivory of netsuke quality in a whole tusk. Dealers and agents who furnish ivory to their carvers often buy netsuke ivory from shops or manufacturers of chopsticks, jewelry, flowers, and other ivory articles. Since these items do not require top-grade ivory, the good ivory can be saved and resold for netsuke carving.

Some merchants import ivory and hire carvers to produce all kinds of ivory pieces: jewelry, flowers, fruit, *okimono*, and other decorative pieces, as well as netsuke, for their own shops in Japan or to sell to other local or foreign dealers. All ivory must be hand-carved, and every carver has his specialty. All ivory work is done by the carver in his own home, and the merchant-importer has both first-rank artist-carvers and division (*bungyo*) carvers working for him.

The latter carvers are craftsmen—many of them highly skilled—who make the inexpensive netsuke found in shops and stores all over the world, as well as in shops throughout Japan. These netsuke, usually carved from models supplied by the employer, lack the originality and the time-consuming, meticulous attention to detail that are found in the first-rank carvers' work. But they are hand-crafted, typical Japanese mementos that the tourist, the person not yet "hooked" on serious netsuke collecting, or someone who cannot afford the higher cost of the better contemporary netsuke, can easily carry, keep, handle, and enjoy.

WORKMANSHIP

Japan is a small, insular country. The prewar Japanese were generally small-boned and small in stature. Their penchant for artistic expression on a small scale and their digital skill can readily be seen in the development of such art forms as sword furniture and netsuke carving.

Toggles and handicraft articles somewhat similar to netsuke have been found in other countries, but the scrupulous, skillful workmanship and the delicate and precise carving of netsuke are virtually unknown outside of Japan.

Time meant little to the early carver. Days, weeks, or months went into the making of a netsuke masterpiece. As any craftsman knows, the task of reducing elaborately ornate or abstractly simple designs to an incredibly small scale requires infinite patience and time as well as great skill and talent. Unfortunately, with the extremely high cost of living in Japan today, time is no longer an expendable component of netsuke making. Due to pressures from dealers and economic demands, occasionally there is quite a spread in the quality of the work from a first-rank carver. In short, in addition to his first-rate netsuke (which may include true masterpieces) there may be pieces that obviously have taken considerably less time to produce or for other reasons are below the capability of the carver.

Two questions are often asked by collectors or potential collectors: "Does the contemporary carver use any power tools for rough work or for polishing?" and "How does the workmanship of a first-rate netsuke carved today compare with that of antique netsuke?"

A few first-rank carvers today own dental drills which they use very sparingly on less than ten percent of their total work. A few also make limited use of an electric polisher. In this connection, it must be remembered that over one hundred years ago some netsuke carvers employed lathes, although these tools were simple and rough. The majority of living carvers use no power tools; they carve with self-made tools and hand-polish their netsuke. The various facets of the workmanship involved in the making of a netsuke will be explored in detail in the following chapter.

Comparison of contemporary and antique netsuke involving comparable techniques will compel even the most prejudiced antique-netsuke collector to admit that the workmanship of some of today's first-rank carvers is fully as admirable as that of the early masters. The absence of functional restrictions often takes a contemporary carver into highly imaginative, intricate designs, involving delicate, exquisite workmanship and the display of craft techniques that cut across various traditional professional schools.

The world in which the netsuke carver lives today is very different from the world of the old masters. But the spirit and the technical skill of the early carvers is splendidly alive in the first-rank contemporary carvers.

TYPES OF NETSUKE

Netsuke, when classified by type, or form, can be broadly divided into the following groups:

1. *Katabori,* or figure carving: the miniature reproduction of either natural objects (people, animals, flowers, insects) or man-made objects (boats, musical instruments, games).

2. *Manju:* the second largest group and probably the earliest form, named for the small rice cake or bun that it resembles. Generally, it is flat and round, although sometimes oval or rectangular. A *manju* may be in one single piece, or it may be divided into two halves that fit into each other, with an additional design on the inside. A variant of the *manju* is the *kagamibuta,* or mirror lid. It is round and bowl-shaped; is usually made of ivory, bone, horn, or wood; and has a metal-disc insert, in most cases made by a famous metal artist. Another variant of the basic *manju* is the *ryusa,* named for an eighteenth-century artist who originated the type. The surface is pierced, and the core has been removed. The outside is usually elaborately carved in a spherical, round, rectangular, or oval shape.

3. *Sashi:* an elongated netsuke, simple in design, five to seven inches in length, with a cord hole in one end.

There are other variant netsuke types, as described in books listed in the Bibliography, but they will not be discussed here because a great majority of contemporary netsuke fall into the *katabori* classification. Occasionally a *manju* made by a living carver appears on a dealer's shelf, but this type of netsuke, even though often exquisite in workmanship, has never been as popular with collectors as the *katabori* type.

MARKETING

A netsuke carver traditionally has an agent, a sponsor, or a dealer. Often the relationship combines all three. In the trade, the term "dealer" is used to designate the individual or firm that acts as the prime outlet for a carver's work. This "dealer" may be a wholesaler and may sell his artist's work to a number of retailers, directly or through monthly auctions. He may also export netsuke. In one or two cases, a wholesale dealer has shops of his own where the work of his artists is featured. Some retail merchants have a quasi-exclusive arrangement for a carver's netsuke, the majority of which will be sold to their own customers. Any surplus will be released to other retailers, either through personal deals or through auction.

Only occasionally does a carver sell directly to different retailers, and seldom, if ever, does he sell directly to a collector. Many practical considerations plus questions of ethics prevent direct dealings between carvers and collectors.

Under the old apprenticeship system, a carver worked with and for his master or his "school" under a master-apprenticeship contract. Such an arrangement could last from fourteen months to fourteen years before the pupil-carver became independent, during which time all of his work was sold by his master or his school. This rigid system is gone, although traces of it remain. The young pupil today may go to the master's house to learn to carve. After working with him for two years and helping him in different ways, he then may be paid a very small amount while continuing his training. But few carvers now work under such a master. The usual carver learns from his father, his uncle, or his grandfather.

Today there are many fringe benefits, as well as some disadvantages, for the carver who markets his work through one prime dealer. This dealer directs his carving schedule to some degree and occasionally supplies design suggestions. Some of the carvers, particularly the younger group, object to this phase of the dealer-carver relationship. Like all artists, and especially young ones, they want to be free to develop their own creative ideas without undue influence or direction.

On the plus side of the relationship, the dealer supplies the carver with ivory and other basic materials. He encourages and helps to develop the promising young carver not yet established. He helps the carver with his tax reports and often assists with the financing of a new home or an addition to an old one. He may take the carver on annual holidays or may assist with the education of his children. He pays him for his work when it is finished, but he may carry it in stock for six months or a year before it is sold. He provides a continuity of market, not only for the living carver but also for generations of carvers to come. Seiichiro Sunamoto, in particular, has encouraged talented carvers, when their work merits emphasis and exposure, by holding special exhibitions of their work, together with illustrated and explanatory catalogues.

One problem in the dealer-carver relationship has always plagued artists. Customarily, certain prices were established for one-figure netsuke of an individual carver and a higher price for his multiple-figure netsuke. Similarly, in Japan a painter, before he has "arrived," is usually paid according to the size of a painting, regardless of its merit. In an art that involves such time-consuming attention to detail as netsuke carving does, and in an era of such incredible escalation in living costs, the problem of paying enough to encourage a talented carver to produce masterpieces and to frequently create new designs is a real one but one that is gradually being solved. The talent and skill of some of the living carvers is so great that it cannot be suppressed in repetitive mediocrity. The dealer, moreover, is beginning to realize that knowledgeable collectors of contemporary netsuke are aware that all work of even the best carvers is not equal in quality and that they are willing to pay a premium for the highest-grade pieces.

As the market for exceptional contemporary pieces spreads throughout the world and the carvers are fairly compensated for netsuke that require unusual skill and time to produce, the quality and continuity of the art of netsuke carving will be assured.

CARVERS

The netsuke carver (*netsuke-shi*) of old Japan was usually ignored, while emphasis was placed on his work. In turn, his work did not receive, in the Japanese world of art, the recognition that it merited. When Western collectors became intrigued with netsuke, books began to appear on the subject, but information about the personal lives of the great carvers was extremely meager. We do know, however, that as a class they were hard-working, dedicated, single-minded, talented men. The Japanese sometimes tell a story of one of the early carvers who built himself a huge "basket," the inside of which was dark except for one little hole. Here he would work by the tiny bit of light filtering through the hole, undisturbed by mundane matters.

It is hard to picture contemporary carvers living a similar life of selfless dedication in the bustling, burgeoning life of Japan today. But they do. The older carvers, who have passed the threescore-and-ten mark, sit in traditional style on the floor, looking out on a tiny, beautiful Japanese garden, dressed in clothing from an earlier era, working on the little embryo netsuke. Patiently, serenely, with self-made tools, they bring the design to life. The room, with its ever present cabinet of little dolls, religious objects, and ceramic pieces, is used for living and often for dining. A TV set, a radio, or a modern clock may inject an incongruous note of today. Over the years, the carvers have adjusted to the harassment of crowded conditions, the cacophony of urban streets, the demands of family life—the centuries-old problem of all artists. They often work from sunrise until sunset, a custom established in earlier days before the carver had the help of artificial light. Carving is their life.

The younger carvers live and work in similar surroundings. Most of them live in or near Tokyo and are faced with establishing a home in a highly inflated economy. The houses are small and crowded, and the carver seldom has a separate workroom. The thin walls do not insulate him from the distracting noises of everyday life in today's Japan: the hum of a sewing machine, the whang of a teen-ager's guitar, the harsh outside noises of motor bikes, trucks, and trains. It is not surprising that many carvers list fishing as their chief hobby. Several of the first-rank carvers have moved from urban districts to outlying or country areas where living is less frenetic, and rentals, property costs, and taxes are lower. Several leading carvers in the Kyoto–Uji–Gifu area have larger homes and enjoy the luxury of a studio on a separate floor, the dream of all carvers.

The younger carvers as a rule try to hold their workday to eight or nine hours instead of the ten-to-twelve-hour day that is the custom of most of the older ones. Ordinarily, the older carvers can be found at their workbenches seven days a week, but the younger carvers are more inclined to set aside one day a week for rest. On that day they may find their relaxation on the golf course or in traveling, visiting, or fishing.

The tempo of industrial Japan today is shut out of the netsuke carver's workroom, regardless of his surroundings and living conditions. Speed has no place in the art of netsuke carving. To capture natural beauty or detailed stories or involved humorous situations in a diminutive piece of sculpture often requires weeks of patient, skilled work. Even though today's first-rank netsuke carvers earn many times what carvers earned decades ago, it is surprising that most of them have not succumbed to the lure of steady and often higher income in the industrial world.

Among the younger carvers is a group that is breaking with tradition— not in quality of work, not in subject matter, but in design. In some cases, the design may take the form of an amusing, enchanting abstract or fantastic rabbit or *shishi* (Figs. 26, 27), or perhaps a swan or a Dutchman (Figs. 13, 112).

The feeling of a traditional netsuke has been maintained, but the designs are completely fresh and innovative. In fact, they are more than that. They are exciting and dynamic. Other artist-carvers may adhere more closely to the traditional approach to legend and history but take advantage of the lack of formal restrictions and produce beautiful pieces of miniature sculpture (Figs. 38, 49, 86). In all cases, however, these netsuke are distinctly Japanese, unlike some of the contemporary Japanese paintings and woodblock prints that are international in essence.

The question is frequently asked, "Are there any women carvers?" The most famous of all women netsuke carvers was Bunshojo, daughter of Tomiharu, the founder of the Iwami school. She lived and worked in the late eighteenth and early nineteenth centuries and was famous for her delicate carving of insects and of long inscriptions on boar-tusk netsuke. Masako Ogura, who learned carving from her father, was a well-known carver in the early part of the twentieth century but produced mostly *okimono*. Many authorities consider her the leading *okimono* carver of her time.

Today, quite a number of women between the ages of fifty and sixty are carving netsuke of inferior quality, doing coloring, polishing, and rough carving, as well as working on ivory jewelry, flowers, and vegetables. The wife of Yukimasa does all of her husband's staining, coloring, and polishing.

Chieko Makino, now in her early thirties, showed considerable promise with her bird netsuke but became ill and stopped carving. Ritsuko Suzuki, daughter of Gyokudo, is very young but is already doing *okimono* finishing work. Mitsuko Suzuki (no relation to Ritsuko), a pupil of Hodo's several years ago, is now doing rough carving. Itsu Seiki wanted to be a carver because her husband was a carver. He had started to teach her to carve before his death in 1969. Today she is working and studying to be a carver of netsuke and *okimono*. With the women of today striving so hard for recognition in fields dominated by men, one can hope that a first-rank woman netsuke carver will emerge soon.

The living carvers, old and young, are now fashioning beautiful netsuke for a worldwide collectors' market rather than for Japanese attire. But they are working with the same warm creativeness, the skill, the patience, the fanatical attention to detail, and the almost religious dedication to their art that characterized the master carvers of earlier centuries. Their netsuke represent a fusion of the traditional art of old Japan with the vitality of new Japan and their own skill and originality.

CHAPTER 3

Subject Matter

SUBJECTS

Since netsuke subject matter covers such a vast area in the imaginary as well as the actual world of the Japanese, it is somewhat difficult to categorize, and any tabulation will involve gaps and overlapping. Broadly, netsuke subjects may be classified as follows:

Folklore, Legend, and History. This area, both in antique and in contemporary netsuke, has always been extremely popular. Some of the tales frequently represented in netsuke art appear later in this chapter.

Nature. Animals form the largest group in this category. They include the animals of the Oriental zodiac, represented either separately or as a complete group of twelve (Fig. 7), as well as otters, squirrels, deer, snails, frogs, and foxes, among others (Figs. 4–26). Birds include the crane, the quail, the stork, the phoenix, the hawk, the mandarin duck, the swan, and the crow (Figs. 10, 13, 20). Among insects are the cicada (Fig. 17), the fly, the locust, the butterfly, and the wasp. Sea creatures include the clam, the octopus, the crab, the cuttlefish, and the blowfish (Figs. 4, 19).

Occupations, Mores, and Customs. The field here is a broad one, and among the types represented we find farmers (Fig. 101), merchants (Fig. 96), craftsmen and artisans (Fig. 100), samurai (Fig. 87), blind masseurs (Fig. 105), dancers (Figs. 78, 79), actors, puppeteers, vendors, calligraphers, fishermen (Figs. 102, 103), sumo wrestlers (Figs. 106, 107), and washers of Buddhist images (Fig. 117).

Religious Figures. These include the Seven Gods of Good Fortune, particularly Hotei (Figs, 51, 58–62, 99); Buddhist patriarchs and deities, particularly Daruma and Kannon (Figs. 113–15); the Sixteen Rakan (Fig. 63); miscellaneous deities (Figs. 119, 120); the Nio; abbots; and mendicants (Fig. 88).

Masks. The masks depicted in netsuke are generally those of the traditional dramatic forms: Bugaku, Kyogen, and Noh. Masks are often used to dramatize ethical concepts.

64

Foreigners. The manners and mores of foreigners, which to the Japanese meant Europeans, particularly the Portuguese, sometimes the Dutch, were often ridiculed in netsuke (Fig. 112).

Miscellaneous, Including Netsuke with Secondary Function. In this area we find seals, musical instruments, family crests, games (Figs. 98, 99), ashtrays, hourglasses, candlesticks, compasses, flints for striking fire, *soroban* (abacuses), whistles, and various toys (Fig. 92).

So-called trick netsuke also appeared in various subjects: the squat Daruma with weighted base to return it always to an upright position; the *karashishi* (Chinese lion) with ball in the mouth; a chestnut with a movable worm; a top-heavy figure that can balance on one foot (Fig. 79); a figure with revolving eyes and protruding tongue; a wasp nest with movable grubs; a pod with movable seeds. The technical skill involved in this kind of netsuke is incredible.

Many contemporary netsuke have moving parts, particularly removable masks, moving heads, and reversible faces. An innovation of the twentieth century, the reversible face usually symbolizes good and evil, or youth and old age, and is analogous to the *yin-yang* concept frequently found in Chinese art. This type of netsuke particularly appeals to the novice collector or to the tourist looking for a Japanese memento.

SOURCES

Since many netsuke subjects are based on Chinese fairy tales and legends, the question is often raised as to whether or not the netsuke is of Chinese origin. Authorities differ concerning this matter. Certainly the custom of toggle wearing prevailed for centuries in most northern countries where men wore robes without pockets, and Chinese decorative toggles undoubtedly predated Japanese netsuke. While both were basically functional, the use of the Chinese toggle as an amulet was as important as its use as a toggle. This is seen in the selection of materials believed to have curative properties and in the designs symbolizing health, longevity, good luck, wealth, or fertility.

Functional requirements were observed in the netsuke, of course, and symbolism in both material and design was not uncommon. However, in keeping with the Japanese tradition that useful things should be beautiful, and beautiful things useful, the aesthetic qualities of the netsuke became all-important.

The peaceful years of the Edo period, when Japan was virtually closed to the rest of the world, saw the development of true Japanese art without further foreign influence. Earlier, various Japanese art forms had been influenced by the art of Korea, India, and particularly China. By the beginning of the Edo period, in the early seventeenth century, the religious, folklore, and other Chinese elements introduced by Buddhist disciples had become absorbed into the life and lore of Japan. When representations of these tales appear in netsuke, they have become distinctly Japanese.

EXPRESSION

Students of netsuke art are always astonished at the ability of the carvers to convey so much in so little. Whole stories or situations are compressed into a diminutive piece of sculpture, often with the carver's own farcical touch or subtle sense of humor. Fearsome legendary monsters become amusing, and great dramas of history become understandable events to which the average Japanese can relate. Humor is often apparent in netsuke design, sometimes even to the point of caricaturing sacred and religious figures. Eroticism also has its place in netsuke design, although nudity is found as rarely in netsuke as in other forms of Japanese art. The eroticism of netsuke art is quite subtle and lighthearted, and it is hardly obvious to the uninitiated.

INDIVIDUALITY

Very little is known of the early carvers. It is only through a study of their netsuke—the subjects they chose, their approach to those subjects, their techniques, and even their choice of materials—that we can get a glimpse of them as human beings and as individuals. Today, when we can meet and know the carvers, we realize how their netsuke reflect not only their background and training but also their characters, their personal interests, their desires: the quiet, restrained softness of a Yoshiyuki (Fig. 52); the love of animals in a Kangyoku (Figs. 8, 9, 11, 14, 15, 23); the warmth and humanness in the Ichiro historical figures (Figs. 82, 88); the childlike love of imaginary animals in a *kappa* netsuke by Ryoshu (Fig. 29); a feeling for the humble person in everyday life in a Hodo (Figs. 92, 102, 104); the love of classical beauty and manners from other eras in a Ryushi (Fig. 49); the breadth of interest in life, legend, and nature in a Meigyokusai (Fig. 32), a Sosui (Fig. 33), or a Masatoshi (Fig. 34).

36. YOUNG PRIEST, BELL, AND ONI. Ivory. Signed: Shogetsu. Date: 1950–60. This netsuke represents an *oni* who, in flagrant violation of regulations, has been smoking in a temple. When a young student priest comes to clean the temple, the *oni* hides under the big bell so he will not be caught. The second part of this dual netsuke, hidden under the bell, shows an *oni* seated with a pipe in his left hand and with the bowl of the pipe held in his right hand. This is an example of Shogetsu's art at its best—an imaginative, intricately carved, and beautifully finished netsuke. (Enlargement: 2.0 times)

67

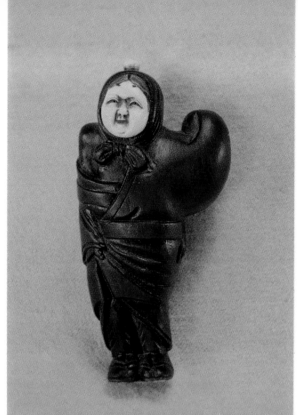

37. HAPPY OKAME: KAGURA DANCE. Wood and ivory. Signed: Yuko. Date: 1971. Here Okame is in the dress and posture of a Kagura dancer. Okame, the goddess of mirth, is frequently found in Japanese art with puffed-out cheeks and a smiling face, a small mouth, a narrow forehead with two ornamental black spots, and hair parted in the middle and brought down over the temples. Yuko has pleasingly combined wood and ivory in this netsuke carved in traditional form. (Enlargement: 1.4 times)

38. HANA-SAKA JIJII. Ivory (antique gold *ojime* on cord). Signed: Shodo. Date: 1965–70. Hana-Saka Jijii is an old man who figures in a popular children's story, in which the ghost of a faithful dog instructs the old man, his former master, to sprinkle dead trees with the ashes of a magical mortar. The trees are immediately covered with blossoms, and the old man becomes famous as he wanders about the countryside magically restoring dead trees to their flowering prime. This carving is more a miniature sculpture than a functional netsuke but, whatever its technical classification, it is a work of superlative merit. (Enlargement: 1.4 times)

Any student of Japanese history, religion, and legend—and all collectors of netsuke eventually become such students—will be able to recognize individual styles, as well as the background and meaning of almost every contemporary netsuke. Identifying these elements is one of the great joys of collecting, and the combination of beauty, individuality, and intriguing subject matter in netsuke art undoubtedly is one of the reasons it has become so popular with collectors throughout the world.

FAVORITE FOLKTALES ILLUSTRATED

In no country in the world can so much of folklore be found in art as in Japan; the netsuke art form is particularly rich in this material. Broadly, folktales are a family of stories originally passed down by word of mouth from generation to generation. Fairy tales form a large segment of this group of stories, and the versions of each tale are as varied as the netsuke designs based upon them. The principal difference between a fairy tale and a legend is that the fairy tale is accepted as fiction and a legend as an account of an actual happening. Both have provided subject matter in profusion for contemporary as well as for antique netsuke.

Certain legendary and fairy-tale characters figure in many stories and are portrayed in several different roles in netsuke art. Ono no Komachi, for example, a ninth-century poet, is very well known as a historical personage, the sole woman among the Six Great Poets of Japan (the Rokkasen). She appears in netsuke art as the legendary heroine of several romantic tales. Netsuke portraying her as Soshi-arai Komachi, or Book-washing Komachi, recall a story in which she clears herself of a charge of plagiarism. A rival poet, according to the legend, copied into an old book a poem he had heard Komachi recite. He then produced the book to prove that the poem was not hers, whereupon Komachi requested some water. When she used the water to wash away the fresh ink, her reputation was completely vindicated (Fig. 64).

The skeleton-and-wolf netsuke is also associated with the celebrated woman poet (Fig. 65). It is thought to allude to the story of Ono no Komachi and the military leader Fukakusa Shosho. Fukakusa died trying to convince Komachi of his love for her. She, living on, suffered the distresses of a solitary old age. The vanity of life is mirrored, for Japanese readers of this story, in the passion of Fukakusa (the wolf) and the pride of Komachi (the skeleton). In old age,

64. Soshi-arai Komachi (Book-washing Komachi).

65. Skeleton and wolf (Komachi and Fukakusa).

Komachi is said to have written, "The flowers have faded without my knowing it, while a long storm kept me indoors."

In a much lighter vein, the badger, or Tanuki, as the animal is called in Japan, is an irresponsible but lovable fairy-tale character whose escapades are amusingly interwoven in tales that touch Japanese daily life. As he is generally portrayed in netsuke and other art, he is wearing a big straw hat and is carrying an IOU pad in one hand and a sakè bottle in the other. Legend says that he would go from bar to bar, paying for his sakè in IOU's. At the end of the year, when all Japanese traditionally settle their outstanding debts, Tanuki, lacking money with which to pick up his numerous IOU's, would turn himself into various objects, often into a teapot. Being rather indolent, he didn't always complete his transformation, and one can occasionally find a teapot in Japan decorated with a badger tail.

In netsuke art, one occasionally finds Tanuki with a lotus-leaf hat, or wrapped in a lotus leaf. One of the many Tanuki tales involves his reformation and his becoming a Buddhist monk. He is often seen in various art forms, particularly in netsuke, with monk's robes and a sanctimonious expression on his face (Figs. 66, 67).

The badger, besides embodying several recognizably human weaknesses, is

Note: The illustrations in this section are sketched from antique and contemporary netsuke.

66. Tanuki with IOU and sakè carafe.

67. Reformed Tanuki, with wooden temple-drum.

one of the animals credited with magical or supernatural powers. Using various disguises, he would often mischievously waylay, deceive, or annoy wayfarers. Standing by the roadside on his hind legs, he would use his distended belly as a drum and strike it with his forepaws. Wrapped in a kimono, he would beg like an itinerant monk, waylay folks crossing paddy fields at night, and cause fishermen to draw up empty nets.

The above examples give some idea of the richness and variety offered by Japanese traditional lore. Those who delve deeper into sources and subject matter will find that many books have been written on the folktales of Japan. There are also a number of books that emphasize the stories particularly used by netsuke carvers. (According to Richard M. Dorson, author of *Folk Legends of Japan,* "in the United States not a single book of legends spoken by the folk has ever been published." Many counterparts of Japanese tales and sayings, however, are found in our own fables and proverbs.) A novice collector will find that a study of the folklore of Japan will add greatly to his appreciation and enjoyment of netsuke.

Obviously, it is impossible to explore this subject extensively in a volume of this kind, but the following are a few examples of favorite fairy tales and legends represented in netsuke art (including one more Tanuki story, a favorite with Japanese children) together with illustrative sketches from both antique and contemporary netsuke.

68. Priest and Bumbuku Chagama.

69. Bumbuku Chagama and priest with water dipper.

BUMBUKU CHAGAMA

Once an antique cauldron was sold to a priest of the Morin-ji temple who liked collecting old curios. One day while he was preparing tea for several of his young apprentice priests, the old cauldron in which he was heating the water began to sizzle and suddenly sprouted a bushy tail, a badger head, and four little badger feet (Figs. 68, 69). Thereupon, it jumped off the fire and began to run around the room. When it was caught, the head, tail, and four little feet disappeared, but the priest was afraid it was a bewitched teakettle and should not be kept around the temple. For a pittance, he sold it to a poor ragpicker who took it home, happy with his bargain.

In the middle of the night the ragpicker was awakened by a shrill voice coming from the cauldron. "Please take care of me and I will help you, for I am Bumbuku Chagama. I am really a badger but took this form to escape cruel boys who were harming me. I don't know what to do with this awkward thing on my back, but I am a lucky cauldron and can do all kinds of tricks. We will start a little theater. People will flock to see me and you will be rich."

Bumbuku's tricks, his tightrope dancing, and his transformations delighted onlookers from far and near. The money poured in, and the ragpicker became rich and was able to have a comfortable house of his own.

One day when the show closed, the ragpicker went backstage to thank his dear friend and found only a cold iron cauldron. The badger had gone.

The ragpicker thought of the old priest who originally had owned the cauldron and, after polishing it, carried it to the temple of Morin-ji with many thanks and half the money earned. There it purportedly rests today on a purple cushion for all to see.

70. Taketori no Okina with infant Kaguya Hime.

THE TAKETORI TALE

One day long, long ago an old bamboo cutter known as Taketori no Okina suddenly became aware of a miraculous light in a bamboo grove and discovered in the heart of a bamboo stem a tiny, exquisite girl only four inches tall. With great gentleness he picked her up and took her home to his wife, who placed her in a basket and happily took care of her (Figs. 70, 71).

After having lived for three months with this simple childless couple, the tiny girl suddenly became full grown and was given the name Kaguya Hime, or Shining Lady. She was the most beautiful of all young women, and the fame of her beauty spread throughout the land. The crowds of would-be husbands, both rich and poor, who came in suit of her hand were finally narrowed down to five wealthy lords and princes.

The bamboo cutter was pressed to choose one of the noble suitors for Lady Kaguya, but he politely explained that she was not really his daughter and could not be compelled to obey his orders.

Lady Kaguya then declared that she could not marry a man who had not proved his love for her, and she devised a plan to test the suitors. Addressing the five men who sought her hand, she said: "In northern India is a beggar's bowl of stone that the Lord Buddha himself carried in ancient times. Let Prince Ishizukuri depart and bring it to me. On the mountain Horai, which towers over the eastern sea, there grows a tree with roots of silver, a trunk of gold, and fruit of pure white jade. I bid Prince Kuramochi to go there and break off and bring me one of its branches. Again, in the land of Morokoshi men make fur robes of the skin of the Flameproof Rat, and I pray the Sadaijin to find me such a robe. Then of the Chunagon I ask that he bring me the rainbow-colored jewel that sparkles deep in the dragon's head, and from the hands of Lord Iso I would like to receive the cowry shell that the swallow carries over the broad plain of the sea."

Prince Ishizukuri decided that instead of going to distant India he would counterfeit the Buddha's begging bowl. After sojourning in the Yamato region for three years, he discovered there an extremely old bowl, wrapped it in brocade, and returned to present it to Lady Kaguya. But she saw instantly that no light shone from the bowl and knew at once that it had never belonged to the Buddha. So the dishonest prince was sent away.

Prince Kuramochi was equally wily. He announced that he was setting out on a journey to the land of Tsukushi in quest of the jewel-bearing branch. Instead of going there, however, he employed six skilled craftsmen to make a branch identical with the one described by Lady Kaguya. Upon presenting it to her, he regaled her with a long and highly imaginative story of his travels and his exploits. She might have believed his clever tale if it had not been for the six craftsmen, who, when he had finished it, appeared on the scene and loudly demanded payment for the imitation jewel-bearing branch. Having been thus exposed, the prince made a hasty retreat, and Lady Kaguya rewarded the six craftsmen.

The Sadaijin was no less crafty. He commissioned a merchant to obtain for him a fur robe made from the skin of the Flameproof Rat. When the merchant's ship returned from the land of Morokoshi, its cargo included a beautiful sea-green fur robe, the hairs tipped with shining gold. It was an incomparably lovely treasure. When the Sadaijin presented it to Lady Kaguya, she ordered it thrown into a bonfire, so that, if it did not burn, she would know that it was indeed made of the skin of the Flameproof Rat and that she would no longer be able to refuse the Sadaijin's suit. A fire was kindled, and the robe was thrown into the flames, where it was immediately consumed. The Sadaijin, astonished to discover that the merchant, like himself, was dishonest, retreated quickly in disgrace.

The Chunagon informed his retainers that he wished them to bring him the jewel from the dragon's head. After showing some hesitancy, they pretended to set off on this mission. Meanwhile, the Chunagon, sure of his retainers' success, had his mansion richly decorated with exquisite lacquerwork in gold and silver. Every room was hung with brocade, and the roof was covered with silken cloths. When, after a reasonable length of time, the retainers did not return, the Chunagon journeyed to the Naniwa region and inquired whether any of them had taken a boat in search of the dragon. Learning that none of them had even come to Naniwa, he himself embarked with a single helmsman.

71. Taketori no Okina finding the baby girl.

After days of high seas and great storms, the boat was near to sinking, and the helmsman advised the Chunagon to offer a prayer for their salvation from this predicament. "My lord," he said, "the screaming of the wind, the anger of the waves, and the mighty roar of thunder are signs of the wrath of the god whom you offend by planning to kill the dragon of the deep." The Chunagon thereupon confessed his folly in seeking to kill the dragon and solemnly swore to leave him in peace and never to return to Lady Kaguya's dwelling. The storm came to an end, and he finally reached home, miserably ill and chilled to the bone. It is said that when the women of his household heard of his adventure they laughed until their sides ached, while the silken cloths that covered the roof of his mansion were carried away thread by thread by crows who used them to line their nests.

The quest of Lord Iso for the cowry shell was equally unsuccessful, and thus the fifth of the wealthy lords and princes was rejected by Lady Kaguya.

By this time the fame of her beauty had reached the court, and the emperor tried many clever devices to induce her to come to his jade palace. When he arrived at her dwelling to press his suit, she suddenly vanished, and the emperor realized that he was not dealing with a mortal woman. He begged her to return, and she once again appeared, just as lovely as before. But the emperor's suit was in vain.

During the seventh month of that year, when the moon was full, Lady Kaguya sorrowfully revealed that she was indeed no ordinary mortal. She told her foster parents that her birthplace was the moon and that the time had come when she must leave the world and return to her home.

At the time of the next full moon, a mysterious and brilliant light shone around the bamboo cutter's house, and a strange cloud came down from the sky bearing a canopied car to carry Lady Kaguya back to the moon. Before she departed, she left a scroll with the heartbroken bamboo cutter and his wife and left another scroll for the emperor, together with some of the magic elixir of life. The scrolls were taken to the summit of Mount Fuji and burned, and for many years the smoke curled up from there to mingle with the clouds.

72. Urashima Taro opening box.

URASHIMA TARO

Reminiscent of the American tale of Rip Van Winkle and of the story of Pandora's box is the Japanese story of Urashima Taro, a poor young fisherman of Mizunoe in the province of Tengu.

Walking on the seashore near his fishing boat, Urashima came upon a group of children who were tormenting a large tortoise. He chased the children away and returned the tortoise to the safety of the ocean. The tortoise was very grateful.

Some days later, when Urashima was fishing far out at sea in his small boat, a sudden storm arose, and he feared he would drown. Just as he was being washed overboard, the tortoise he had befriended appeared and said, "Urashima-san, thank you for your recent kindness to me. I have come to take you to the Ryugu, the palace of the Dragon King." Urashima climbed on the back of the tortoise and soon was gliding through the sea at great speed. As they plunged deeper and deeper into the sea, beautiful fish holding lanterns lighted their way to the entrance to the Dragon Palace, where the lovely daughter of the Sea King, Princess Otohime, waited to greet her visitor. "Dear Urashima," she said, "you have been so kind to my tortoise. Wouldn't you like to spend some time with me in my palace?"

In this magnificent palace, Urashima had fine clothes to wear, hosts of fish servants to wait upon him, and the company of the most beautiful lady he had ever seen. Months and years slipped by, but he never forgot his home or his

73. Urashima Taro aging.

friends. When he thought of them, a shadow would cross his face, and one day the princess asked him what made him look sad. He told her he could not forget his home and friends in the upper world and he thought it was time to bid her farewell. She nodded in understanding and said the faithful tortoise would take him home. He put on his old fisherman's clothes and with a heavy heart went to the princess to thank her and to bid her farewell. As he left, she handed him a black lacquer box and asked that he promise to carry it wherever he went and on no account ever to open it.

He mounted the tortoise's back and they quickly rose through miles of ocean depths. When he recognized familiar scenery, he jumped off the tortoise and ran eagerly toward his father's house. It was gone! Only the little stream remained. He wandered to other houses, but everywhere the streets were strange and the faces unfamiliar. People laughed at his old-fashioned fisher-man's clothes, and no one remembered him. "Doesn't anyone know Urashima, the fisherman?" he kept asking. Finally, an old man said he had heard a strange tale of a youth by that name who over three hundred years before had been seen riding into the sea on the back of a tortoise.

Urashima sat disconsolately on the seashore. All he had left was the box the princess had given him. In spite of her admonition, he opened it. A wisp of smoke rose from it and surrounded him. A sacred promise had been broken, and gradually he turned from a handsome youth into a wrinkled old, old man (Figs. 72, 73). He looked toward the sea and then fell dead upon the shore.

74. Kiyo, Anchin, and the Dojo-ji bell.   75. Dojo-ji bell.

KIYO, ANCHIN, AND THE DOJO-JI BELL

The beautiful Kiyo was the fairest girl in a far-famed teahouse that stood beside a hill near the banks of the Hidaka River. Across the river stood the Dojo-ji, a Buddhist temple with a belfry housing a great bell, six inches thick and weighing several tons.

In the temple, the abbot and the priests lived a devout monastic life. The priests were especially forbidden to stop at teahouses, for fear that they might lose their spirituality. Upon returning from a shrine one day, the priest Anchin saw the pretty Kiyo moving about gracefully in the tea garden. At first he resisted the impulse to speak to her, but, as time went on, his love grew so intense that he broke a temple rule and entered the forbidden teahouse.

After he had been with Kiyo for many nights, Anchin's conscience rose above his passion and, with an ascetic calm, he endeavored to break his relationship with her. She tried with every feminine wile to rekindle his love and, failing, turned her efforts to putting him to death by sorcery.

As Anchin left Kiyo for the last time, he suddenly saw her eyes turn into those of a serpent. Terrified, he swam across the river and hid himself inside the huge temple bell. With her magic, Kiyo transformed herself into a hissing, fire-spitting dragon-serpent, swam across the river, and entered the belfry. The coils of the serpent surrounded the bell until it was red-hot and it rang with the shrieks of the priest. Finally, his voice was heard no more. The bell melted, and with it were destroyed the priest Anchin and the once beautiful Kiyo (Figs. 41, 74, 75).

76, 77. Ono no Tofu and the frog.

ONO NO TOFU AND THE FROG

Calligraphy in both China and Japan was an art in itself, as highly regarded as drawing and painting. It was also a necessary social accomplishment.

Ono no Tofu was a man of high birth whose writing was embarrassingly poor and childlike. One day in spring, he was walking in a suburb of Kyoto when he came to a large willow tree with branches hanging almost to the ground. His attention was drawn to a frog trying to jump to one of the lower branches. The frog could not get a foothold and time after time fell to the ground. Exhausted and panting, he seemed to give up the struggle. But, after resting for a time, he began to jump again with renewed determination, and after several attempts he secured a foothold and made his way up the tree.

Tofu was greatly impressed and took the lesson seriously. He solemnly resolved to make every effort to learn to write properly. So well did he persevere that in a few years he became Japan's most famous calligrapher (Figs. 76, 77).

CHAPTER 4

Collecting Contemporary Netsuke

COLLECTORS

The first question a living carver asks a collector is "But *why* do you want to buy netsuke?" And he waits seriously and intently for the interpreter to convey the answer. These artists sit all day working on a tiny, beautiful art object, infusing it with their spirit. They know a netsuke is no longer a functional part of Japanese attire. They also know that less than ten percent of the netsuke produced today are purchased by Japanese. But they know little about the people who will buy and enjoy them. What is there about a netsuke that completes the cycle of spirit that passes from the artist to the object and in turn to the foreign buyer? What does the collector like? What does he do with the netsuke he collects?

The answers to these questions vary with collectors. My husband and I bought our first netsuke in 1958 from Hirokazu Nakayama, owner of Yamato Brothers in Tokyo. Little did we then realize that we had been bitten by a bug—that we had begun what would develop into an exciting and absorbing but expensive hobby. We have since learned that this first netsuke of ours was carved by Yoko, who, until his death in 1974, was alert and carved every day. At the time, the name of the carver meant nothing to us. Nor did the question of whether it was old or new even occur to us. We knew nothing of the history of netsuke or netsuke carvers. We only knew that we had an enchanting, beautifully carved, typically Japanese piece of miniature sculpture. Now, several hundred netsuke later, it is still one of our most treasured carvings (Fig. 51).

Our subsequent buying contacts took us along the trail of first-rate contemporary netsuke. Our interest grew as we acquired more books on netsuke, on Japanese art and history, and countless volumes dealing with the fairy tales, folklore, and legends of Japan. Inevitably we learned to know and appreciate the older netsuke and have added a number of them to our collection. Within a few years, we were recognizing the names, the techniques, and the characteristic styles of the first-rank contemporary carvers—Ichiro, Hodo, Sosui, Shogetsu. And when we met some of the carvers and saw them at work, a completely new facet was added. We knew then that we were really "hooked" on collecting contemporary netsuke.

Most people are collectors at heart. The particular path down which you will go depends upon many factors: childhood interests, educational background, exposure to various arts and crafts through teachers and friends, and, by no means least, the size of your bank account. You may collect a certain thing at one time of life; then perhaps that interest, for one reason or another, will exhaust itself. But always you will start to collect something else. The collecting disease may be arrested; it is never cured.

THE MOTIVATIONS OF COLLECTORS

Scholarly Interest. The subject matter of netsuke covers every phase of Japanese history, legend, folklore, religion, and everyday life—all recorded by the carver's tools instead of the pen. The materials of netsuke involve a whole area of medical beliefs, religious symbolism, and affinities of certain artists for certain media. The techniques include those of many arts and crafts besides carving: lacquer, metalwork, weaving, inlay, painting, and ceramics. In short, the variety of subject matter, material, and techniques in netsuke takes the student into never ending, ever broadening research in the world of Japanese art and culture—a world of humor, history, and imagination completely fascinating to the observer or knowledgeable collector who can understand the proverbs, the jokes, and the puns or recognize the legendary tales or characters caught by the artist-carvers in their flights of fancy.

Visual, Tactile, and Portable Appeal. To the collector who cares only for that exchange of spirit from artist to object and from object to owner, a netsuke is most satisfying. Few art objects have such eye appeal and are still small enough to handle and fondle. Often a netsuke is carried in a pocket to feel and rub as the Chinese use the "touch" stone. Several can be kept on a small desk or bedside table or can add an Oriental touch to living-room decor. Even a sizable collection can be displayed in a small cabinet.

Often when the sunset years approach and a large home becomes a burden instead of a pleasure, it is difficult to know what to do with paintings and large art treasures that would crowd and overwhelm the small home or apartment chosen for retirement living. Netsuke pose no such problem.

Challenge of Authenticity. The question of authenticity in antique netsuke is as challenging as it is frustrating. Over half of the early netsuke were unsigned, and pupils often followed their masters closely in design and technique. The signature of the master was frequently used by prize pupils, and under most circumstances there was no stigma attached to the copying of a design—or a signature. It takes a very knowledgeable netsuke scholar and serious study of many netsuke attributed to a certain carver to make possible the spotting of copies or spurious signatures. An interest in a particular artist-carver of the seventeenth, eighteenth, or nineteenth century invariably involves this difficult but fascinating problem of authenticity.

The collector of twentieth-century netsuke can specialize in the work of particular carvers without this problem. All top contemporary carvers sign their netsuke. No longer is there an apprenticeship system nor are there professional schools of carving where designs and signatures are copied. And, as yet, there is little copying of the work of first-rate contemporary carvers.

Investment. Many collectors, admittedly or not, look upon intelligent art collecting as an investment—either for capital gain or as a hedge against inflation. Many fortunes have been made by collectors who acquired their netsuke at comparatively low pre–World War II prices. During the past decade, some of the large collections sold at London auction houses have brought astonishingly big prices, ranging from $100 to $27,000 for a single netsuke.

Scarcity, of course, always plays a decisive part in the value of an art object. The number of authentic antique netsuke in the hands of world collectors has not increased since the turn of this century, except for those which came on the market in Japan during the occupation. On the contrary, some collections have been willed to museums, taking a considerable number out of circulation. The number of collectors, meanwhile, has mushroomed. Most new collectors hoard their top netsuke for some time, further decreasing the "float."

The new collector of antique netsuke finds it difficult and expensive to put together a sizable number of first-rate early netsuke. There are, however, as in most collecting fields, rare and exciting bargains or "sleepers," and the knowledgeable netsuke enthusiast can still put together an enviable collection at a cost that can be returned with reasonable profit at current world prices.

The top contemporary netsuke cannot be purchased for next to nothing, as were the good antique netsuke coming out of Japan in the latter part of the nineteenth century and immediately after World War II. In fact, first-rate contemporary netsuke will cost as much as many good antique netsuke, and the netsuke of a few living carvers sell for prices ranging from $300 to $2,000 each. The number of first-rate netsuke being produced today is comparatively small, and as recognition of their beauty and excellence permeates the world of netsuke collectors, unquestionably they will take their place pricewise beside antique netsuke in world auctions.

Unfortunately, scarcity plays a much larger part than it should—or than most collectors will admit—in the price of an art object. This is evidenced in the prices now commanded by netsuke of some twentieth-century carvers who are ill or for other reasons are nonproductive, or of carvers who have died.

I firmly believe that top contemporary netsuke at current prices, selectively and knowledgeably chosen, are an excellent investment. At least, this is what my husband and I tell each other when we come home from Japan with far more netsuke in our bags than we can afford. However, I might add, we have yet to sell—or even trade—a single contemporary netsuke.

SPECIALIZED COLLECTING

A broad cross section is usually found in large netsuke collections: netsuke by famous carvers of different eras; netsuke of a wide variety of materials, including wood, ivory, metal, lacquer, jade, coral, and ceramic ware; and netsuke on subjects covering every phase of life and culture in Japan.

In smaller collections, the netsuke addict often tends to specialize. One collector in New York collects nothing but netsuke with natural *himotoshi*— netsuke with natural openings in the carving itself, like the branch of a tree, the crook of an arm, or the twist of a dragon's tail, rather than carved holes through which the cord can pass (Fig. 27).

Another collector may look for zodiac animals or perhaps one type of animal—elephants, frogs, or horses—or imaginary animals. Another person may narrow his interest to masks; another to Buddhist images. Some collectors buy only wood netsuke, and others look for those combining two or more materials: ivory and wood, metal and wood, metal and ivory, tortoise shell and ivory, mother-of-pearl and wood, and the like.

An architect might look for netsuke pertaining to his profession. A doctor might have a special interest in stories of medicinal values attributed to different types of wood used in netsuke. He would also look for deerhorn netsuke, scrapings from which were believed to be an effective remedy for snakebite. And he would value a narwhal ivory netsuke with a small area left uncarved so that scrapings from it could be used as an antidote for poison.

Some collectors become specialists in the work of one or more carvers. A Chicago collector has accumulated over thirty Ichiro netsuke. "Personally," he said, "I think that Ichiro does about the finest job of any of the carvers in giving his little people real character. One feels that his people can almost talk. And if they could, wouldn't they have interesting tales to tell!"

One of the great pleasures of netsuke collecting is to become a member of the circle of interesting collectors and dealers throughout the world whose paths inevitably cross. In our area in California, small groups of collectors periodically get together for a show-and-tell party. The excitement of sharing new acquisitions and netsuke knowledge with fellow collectors is unquestionably one of the reasons a netsuke-collecting hobby seldom exhausts itself. It may extend to other Japanese art forms, but, usually, once a netsuke collector, always a netsuke collector.

NOTES FOR NOVICES

Once you have been exposed to the charm of a netsuke, and perhaps have acquired two or three, you may ask, "Where do I go from here? How do I know a really good netsuke from a mediocre one?"

My initial advice would be to follow your own taste, your own artistic instinct. Buy a netsuke because it strikes a responsive chord in you. Perhaps you are attracted by the sheer beauty of the design and workmanship or perhaps the subject matter has particular appeal. It is then a "good" netsuke for you.

Don't try to digest in a short time all that has been written on netsuke. You may find yourself in a discouraging jungle of matters involving authenticity, the incredible disparity in prices, and countless other confusing aspects of netsuke collecting. Rather, let your purchases take you gradually into the study of netsuke, with emphasis on your particular areas of interest. Whenever possible, examine and study netsuke in museums, in private collections, and at showings before auction sales. Eventually the problems will become challenges, and your interest in netsuke will expand from the emotional, artistic motiva-

tion to a knowledgeable interest in the carvers, certain phases of subject matter and media, and perhaps even to the investment aspect. As you become more knowledgeable, you will become more selective.

If you are going to become a serious collector, there are certain basic criteria to look for. These differ somewhat in antique and contemporary netsuke. The patina of age and wear so desirable in antique netsuke is, of course, absent from new, nonfunctional netsuke. Likewise, the quality and variety of materials is not a matter of great concern to buyers of contemporary netsuke. At least eighty percent of the netsuke being carved today are made of ivory, and the artist-carver who spends fifty to one hundred and seventy-five hours on a single netsuke will use only prime, top-grade ivory.

For the serious netsuke antiquarian, the problem of authentication is fascinating but difficult and often frustrating. It is a never ending study, since there are some twenty-five hundred known signatures of early carvers and many thousands of unsigned netsuke. The collector of contemporary netsuke has only the challenge of learning to recognize the work and signatures of roughly fifteen to twenty first-rank carvers and twenty to thirty in the second rank. All sign their work, and the majority of them have definite and easily recognizable characteristics of design and workmanship.

The collector of antique netsuke looks for the functional requirements that were as much a part of the early netsuke as the aesthetic qualities. As a toggle worn at the girdle, the netsuke had to be smooth, usually with rounded corners, and so designed that it could not be broken easily. The cord holes had to be placed so as not to impair the design of the visible portion of the netsuke and fashioned so as to permit the cords to pass through the holes easily. Some collectors look for these attributes in contemporary netsuke. Most living carvers follow the old guidelines of the functional netsuke. Some feel, however, that since netsuke are, in fact, no longer functional, there is no reason to restrict designs by considerations of utility. The result would be called a miniature *okimono* or a piece of diminutive sculpture by the netsuke purist. The question is merely academic. Whether netsuke or miniature sculpture, it can be a delight to the connoisseur or collector.

First-rate netsuke are often displayed among quickly produced pieces of mediocre quality. But the disparity in the artist's skill and the time spent on the good netsuke are reflected in their prices. Usually the good netsuke are priced three to five times higher than those of poor quality.

A novice collector quickly learns to look for the degree of care and skill shown in carving the features of the face, the hands, and the feet. This is one of the easiest ways to spot a good netsuke. There is, as well, a feeling in the work of a master carver that he has carved "in," not "on," the ivory.

There is an easily perceptible difference in the finish of a first-rate netsuke—the polish, the staining or coloring, the meticulous attention to detail. Sometimes too much color or stain is used. This tends to diminish the subtlety and charm of the netsuke and may cover a defect in the ivory. The color sometimes fades and wears off as the years go by. Moreover, the highly colored netsuke lacks the tactile quality of an uncolored netsuke, since it cannot be fondled.

Unless several materials are combined in a carving, a good netsuke is made from a single piece of ivory, wood, or other material. Designs are sometimes quite intricate, and much time can be saved by carving some of the parts separately and then joining them with glue or cement. Difference in the color of the wood or the grain in the ivory or excessive use of color or stain at a logical welding place is usually a clue that separate parts have been joined.

The tourist or casual buyer looking for a typically Japanese memento will find that many of the less expensive netsuke done by amateurs and less skilled artists can have charm or humor or sentimental value. Such a netsuke may perhaps give as much pleasure to its owner as a first-rate carving gives to the sophisticated collector. And it can lead one into the exciting world of netsuke collecting.

SIGNATURES

Even though many of the finest antique netsuke are unsigned, the signed piece has always brought a higher price in the marketplace than the unsigned piece of comparable quality. Learning to recognize the work and signatures of leading netsuke artists is exciting and rewarding to the sophisticated collector. To the novice, it can be confusing and even discouraging. The many ramifications of this part of the netsuke world are covered in *The Netsuke Handbook of Ueda Reikichi* and other books. In this chapter, only points pertinent to signatures of contemporary carvers will be touched upon (see Appendix 1).

During the Edo period (1603–1868) the use of surnames was limited to the nobility and the samurai except when special permission was granted by the lord of a fief. The netsuke of this period were usually signed with the carver's *go* (professional or art name). The *go* was given to a worthy pupil by his master and usually contained a portion of the teacher's name. After the Restoration in 1868, the use of surnames was freely permitted regardless of social rank. Since that time, carvers have had surnames as well as professional names and occasionally will use both, especially when there is more than one carver with the same professional name. The majority of contemporary carvers, however, sign only with their *go*.

Through the custom of being given the privilege of using a portion of the master's name in their *go*, many living carvers can be traced to earlier masters. The following are examples: Tomochika (1800–1873), Nobu*chika*, *Nobu*yuki, *Nobu*yoshi, *Yoshi*yuki (1893–1970); Komei, *Mei*do, Ko*do*, Ho*do*; Gyokuzan (1843–1923), Sho*zan*, *Sho*gin, Mei*gin* (Meigyokusai).

Some contemporary carvers use one name when carving netsuke and another name on *okimono*—for example, Toshitake Nakamura uses the name Yuko on his netsuke and the name Somei on *okimono* (p. 233).

In earlier days, the carver sometimes used different names at different periods of his life. This custom is seldom followed today, although the great Kyoto carver Meigyokusai was known as Meigin (and occasionally used the signature Toshitsugu) until he was seventy. At that time, he took the name Meigyokusai, which he had used before the war on *okimono* (p. 224). He is also a noted poet, and when he writes *senryu* verses, he uses the pen name Koju.

One carver from Gifu City uses three different signatures: Yukimasa on his best netsuke, Masatomo on his "middle" work, and Tomoichi on his animals, the last after the early carver of animal netsuke from the Gifu area (p. 233).

The late Yoko (Komada) always used the name Kyokusen on work he produced for Shigeo Tsujita, his very good friend and longtime agent for several leading carvers.

A skillful contemporary carver by the name of Kogyoku uses four different signatures: Kogyoku on his first-quality and second-quality netsuke, but with different characters; Masatoshi on his third-quality netsuke; and on netsuke he rates last, the name Yuji (p. 222).

For the most part, however, the question of signatures and authenticity in the case of first-quality contemporary netsuke is a simple one. Virtually all are signed; most are signed with the artist's professional name; and usually each carver has such a definite style and technique that it doesn't take long to learn to identify his netsuke without even looking at the signature.

COPIES IN NETSUKE ART

Netsuke collecting inevitably brings the buyer into the bewildering jungle of the philosophy of "copies in art," which in turn leads to the basic question "What is a work of art?" James Michener, in his *Japanese Prints from the Early Masters to the Modern,* answers this question by saying, in part: "First, a work of art must exist as an idealistic concept in the mind of a human being. . . . It is generated from an intuitive impulse. . . . The second requirement of a work of art is its realization in some objective form which the human audience can perceive."

The netsuke art form, probably more than any other, raises confusing questions as to the ethics of copying and as to whether a copy can be a work of art. In Japan, a stigma has never been attached to a carver's copying his master's netsuke designs or those of other carvers. In fact, the master often prepared pages of sketches for the pupil to follow. Frequently a young artist who produced an exceptionally fine netsuke would honor his master by using the master's signature and thus forgo credit for his own skill.

As did artists in almost all forms, the early netsuke artist-carver often repeated, with slight variations, a popular original design. This custom is also followed by most contemporary netsuke carvers. The frequent repetition of a popular design, without variation, is a practice dealers should not encourage and carvers should avoid. Picasso once said: "Success is dangerous. One begins to copy oneself, and to copy oneself is more dangerous than to copy others. It leads to sterility."

Occasionally a contemporary artist-carver is asked to make an exact copy of an antique netsuke. He has no scruples about doing so, although he would prefer a commission to carve a netsuke of his own design. In copying an old netsuke, a contemporary netsuke carver executes someone else's "intuitive impulse," perhaps even more skillfully than did the original carver. If the collector is more of an appreciator of art than a serious antiquarian, he can accept such a netsuke as a beautiful piece of miniature sculpture conceived by a fine artist of the seventeenth, eighteenth, or nineteenth century and carved by a modern craftsman.

However, sometimes a copy of an old netsuke, carved by a contemporary artist, is sold as an authentic antique. This is a *caveat emptor* situation for the collector—a common one. The art collector, from time immemorial, and in almost every art form, has been plagued by the existence of copies of the work of noted masters, sold as originals.

As previously noted, the authenticity of contemporary netsuke has not posed much of a problem for the collector. However, the limited supply of first-quality contemporary netsuke and the high prices they command have apparently given rise to the production of some copies by Hong Kong carvers. The knowledgeable, experienced buyer should have little trouble spotting such spurious pieces. The novice collector must beware and seek dealers who can be trusted.

DEALERS

Where can top-quality contemporary netsuke be purchased? London has traditionally been the capital of the netsuke world market. Most of the original large collections in Europe—chiefly in London and Paris—reached second-generation collectors, either directly or indirectly, through London auction sales during the first quarter of the twentieth century. Glendining and Company, with Henri Joly, an outstanding Oriental art authority, as a firm member, handled most of the large netsuke sales of this period. Subsequently, Christie's and Sotheby's came into the London netsuke-auction picture; Parke-Bernet dominated the New York scene, as the Hôtel Drouot dominated Paris; galleries handling Oriental art mushroomed in Germany and elsewhere throughout the world. Today, Sotheby's, which acquired Parke-Bernet in 1964, and Christie's have established auction houses or sales offices in most of the large cities on five continents. In 1969, both firms held sales in Tokyo for the first time, and in 1970 Sotheby's opened a large and beautiful establishment in Beverly Hills, California. Since World War II, Sotheby's in London has handled the most important netsuke sales, including that of the M. T. Hindson collection.

Until Christie's and Sotheby's held auctions in Tokyo, Japanese art auctions were open only to dealers. Elsewhere in the world, most auctions are open to individuals as well. Netsuke collectors may bid in person or by mail through catalogue numbers. Dealers bid for their own stock, or they may do commission buying for collector-clients unable to attend the auction. Small dealers seldom bid at important netsuke auctions, since they feel that they cannot compete against the large dealers for the good pieces. They rely on purchases from individual collectors or occasionally trade or buy from other dealers. Both large and small dealers add to their stock through private-estate purchases and through netsuke turned over to them on consignment by collectors.

A few first-rate contemporary netsuke by Sosui, Masatoshi, Keiun, and Kangyoku occasionally appear in auction catalogues. In the United States and Europe, reliable dealers, knowledgeable in the field of antique netsuke, are becoming increasingly interested in adding first-rate netsuke by living carvers to their inventories, and jewelry sections of large metropolitan department stores now and then display good twentieth-century netsuke. For example, late in 1970 a group of excellent contemporary netsuke, including several by Keiun, were featured in the jewelry department of Bullock's-Wilshire, Beverly Hills, California. Arcade shops featuring Oriental art found in large hotels such as the Plaza in New York and the Century Plaza in Los Angeles display quite a number of netsuke, the majority of which are mediocre contemporary pieces. The practiced eye, however, can usually spot the first-rate pieces among them. The number of fine contemporary netsuke in the better shops is steadily increasing. In almost every city in the United States gift shops carrying Oriental items will have a few netsuke, usually good to poor contemporary pieces. In general, the better the shop, the better the netsuke.

While London still is considered the top marketplace for antique netsuke, Tokyo is the capital of the contemporary netsuke world. It should be noted, however, that some of the finest contemporary pieces can be found today in Hawaii, throughout the continental United States, and in Europe.

The large hotels in Tokyo and other metropolitan cities in Japan all have ivory or gift shops where the work of one or more top living carvers is featured. Also displayed in these shops are countless contemporary netsuke of lesser quality. Antique shops will frequently have a few first-quality contemporary netsuke in addition to antique pieces, and shops featuring contemporary Japanese crafts will usually display netsuke. Most of the large department stores—Takashimaya, for example—carry both antique and contemporary netsuke.

But what of the hundreds, perhaps thousands, who are collectors or potential netsuke buyers and who cannot get to Japan or London or other large art shopping centers? They will learn to watch local auctions, held in most of the larger American cities, for sales including Oriental items. Usually, there are netsuke—some new, some old—of quality ranging from mediocre to excellent. Netsuke collectors always attend presale showings since there are often "sleepers" in such a sale. They will comb little out-of-the-way shops for the occasional treasure. They will learn that good jewelry stores from time to time have a few netsuke, acquired perhaps in an auction or estate purchase. They will hear of some shops in rather unlikely places that specialize in good contemporary netsuke. Upon request, the owners will send pictures of netsuke in a particular area of interest and sometimes mail pieces on approval. For example, Rose and Dan Bowman, owners of Red Torii Antiques in Charleston, South Carolina, carry a sizable stock of first-rate contemporary netsuke. And visitors to the little town of Lahaina, on the island of Maui, in Hawaii, will be surprised to find a stock of netsuke, sixty-five percent of them contemporary, at a shop called The Gallery. This shop, which also features Oriental jade and porcelains, has netsuke customers all over the world.

In a setting as different as it is far from Hawaii, is a farmhouse-gallery of Oriental art in Deep River, Connecticut. It is also the home of its owners, Betty and Walter Killam. A wide variety of Oriental art is displayed, but Betty Killam's great love is netsuke. She is well informed on the subject and carries a sizable stock of excellent contemporary netsuke.

A list—admittedly incomplete—of shops and dealers is included in this volume (see Appendix 4). Those named are known to the author, directly or indirectly, for handling good-quality netsuke, including some first-rate contemporary pieces. Absence of comment means that the author and her husband are not personally familiar with the shop or the dealer.

 Part Two

CHAPTER 5

Techniques

WHETHER they are engaged in research, study, contemplation, drawing, or clay modeling, contemporary carvers perform the same painstaking preliminaries that have always been a time-consuming part of netsuke carving. And the carver still sits on a tatami mat as he works in his small room, or perhaps a corner of a larger room, shutting out the turbulent world from his moments of creation (Fig. 123). Basic methods, too, have changed very little since the earliest years of decorative netsuke carving. Materials, however, have changed somewhat. Very few netsuke are carved in wood today, and the techniques used in carving ivory netsuke are not the same as those used for wood. The discussion of netsuke-carving techniques in this chapter, therefore, will be confined to those of the ivory carver.

TOOLS

Except for the saws and files involved in the first stages of carving a netsuke, the scores of tools used by carvers are usually self-made. Most of the knives (*nomi*) are steel, short-bladed, with long, strong wood handles. Some of the tools are fine and pointed; some are curved like dental tools and are used for etching (Fig. 124). The tool used for roughing the ivory prior to applying color to simulate cloth is called the *arashi* tool, and another is called the "ear-cleaner" tool. In short, there is a tool for each place and each purpose. Meigyokusai says that when he was learning to carve he would choose a carving knife slowly and with hesitancy, but now his hand, like that of a surgeon, instinctively reaches for the proper knife. Ichiro says that if he loses one tool it makes a difference in his carving.

According to Meigyokusai, the netsuke artist usually carves toward his body, but the sculptor of Buddhist images always carves outward. However, Ichiro says he usually carves outward except when doing the right side of the face of a figure; then he carves inward. Kangyoku also usually carves outward, but when the surface is rough, he carves inward.

123. Workbench.

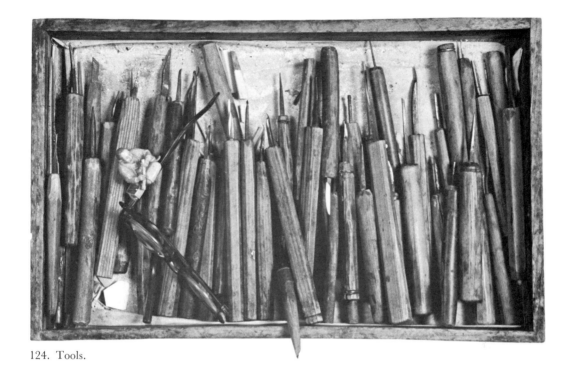

124. Tools.

ROUGH CARVING

A fine-edged handsaw (*nokogiri*) is used to cut an ivory slice from the tusk "point." This piece is used for one, two, or three netsuke depending upon the size of the tusk and the size and design of the netsuke to be carved. The same saw is used to cut off the corners and make the rough shape of the design. This stage is followed by shaving and filing until the rough design emerges. The first file used is a large, flat, one-sided file, generally called a *sharime*, 2 centimeters wide and 20 centimeters long. Next a small *sharime* (.5 to 1 centimeter by 15 centimeters), a clam file (*gangi*), and occasionally a one-sided file called *hira-gangi* or *gangi-hira*, together with a small chisel (*nomi*), are used to develop the design (see Fig. 130e–g). The knives and tools used in subsequent carving stages depend entirely upon the design and the carver. Certain tools are used for the face, others for folds of clothing, and special tools are used if a reversible face or moving parts are involved in the design.

The hand drill (*rokuro*) is still used by many carvers (Fig. 125), although most

135

125. Shofu Amano using a hand-drill (*rokuro*).

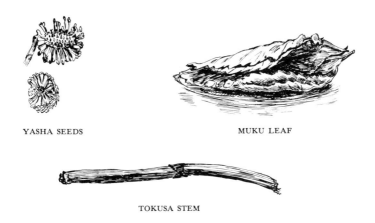

YASHA SEEDS   MUKU LEAF

TOKUSA STEM

126. Materials used for polishing and staining.

of the younger carvers use an electric dental drill when the design calls for small holes or openings in the ivory or when it is difficult to use a file in a tiny corner during the rough-carving stage. Not over five to ten percent of the work is done by such a drill, and it is never used on any of the final carving. Masatoshi uses neither the *rokuro* nor any electric drill. Like all drills, the *rokuro* generates heat as it is being used. Many years ago when Masatoshi's father, Kuya, was using a *rokuro*, it slipped and burned his hand badly. After that accident, neither Kuya nor Masatoshi ever used a drill. Instead, Masatoshi has used a special tool to "push" into the ivory when making holes.

POLISHING, STAINING, AND FINAL CARVING

The polishing of a netsuke takes more energy than any other stage. After the rough shaping and carving have been completed, the carver begins the polishing process, first using a rough stem of *tokusa* grass. This is followed by brushing with polishing powder. Each carver has his favorite polishing powder, and different powders are used for the various stages of the finishing process. Yoshiyuki dried the leaves of the *Aphananthe aspera* and *Equisetum hiemale* plants and crushed them into a powder. Some carvers use the leaf of the *muku* tree (Fig. 126); others use ground deerhorn or very fine sandpaper. *Toishi* powder, which comes from the *toishi* stone, used for sharpening knives, is often used on the final polish.

After the preliminary stages of polishing with *tokusa* or other polishing sticks, brushing with powder, and then rubbing with a cloth and polishing powder, the netsuke is placed in warm *yasha* "soup," where it remains only five to fifteen minutes the first time. This "soup," as the carvers call it, is made by boiling the nuts or seeds of the *yasha* tree for half a day in an earthenware bowl (Fig. 126). Some carvers use other nuts or vegetable seeds to make their staining liquid. After the netsuke is removed from the "soup," it is cooled in cold water. The face, the eyes, the ears, and other details are then carved, and the stain is polished away in the areas that are to be free of it. This procedure is repeated until the desired staining effect has been achieved and the final carving of design details has been completed, as shown in Figure 130(1).

Lastly, hairlines are added with *sumi* ink (Fig. 130 m), and colors are added to mark the inside and outside of the eyes and other design highlights. Tortoise shell or other material is inlaid for the eyes. For the final polishing the carver usually puts *toishi* powder on his fingers and hand-polishes the netsuke.

COLORING

While color on wood netsuke goes back to the early eighteenth century and subsequently there was limited use of color on ivory, the extensive use of paint on ivory netsuke began with Ichiro in the twentieth century. Today almost all living carvers are proficient in the use of color, but some use it only for design accents. There are almost as many variations of color usage as there are carvers.

Ichiro's colors are those used in Japanese painting. They come in sticks that Ichiro dips into water and rubs into a paste on a plate. Shade variations are achieved by mixing various stock colors. He says that before the war he used colors imported from Germany, which were of better quality than those made and sold in Japan today (see Fig. 138).

Ryushi makes his own colors and has more than twenty he now uses. His soft, rosy rust has become almost as much a hallmark as Ichiro's bright blue. He blends bottled watercolor paint with paste or starch. He has found that it is almost impossible for this kind of mixture to come off the ivory or to deteriorate.

Meigyokusai makes his paint by mixing *ganryo* (powdered stone) and varnish. He gets his reds, yellows, and browns from natural earth colors, gold from gold powder, silver from aluminum powder, and purple from stone powder.

The technique used in simulating rough cloth is called *arashi*. The ivory is roughened by the *arashi* tool before the color is applied. The colored netsuke is then placed overnight in a dark, damp place, often the space between the floor of the house and the ground.

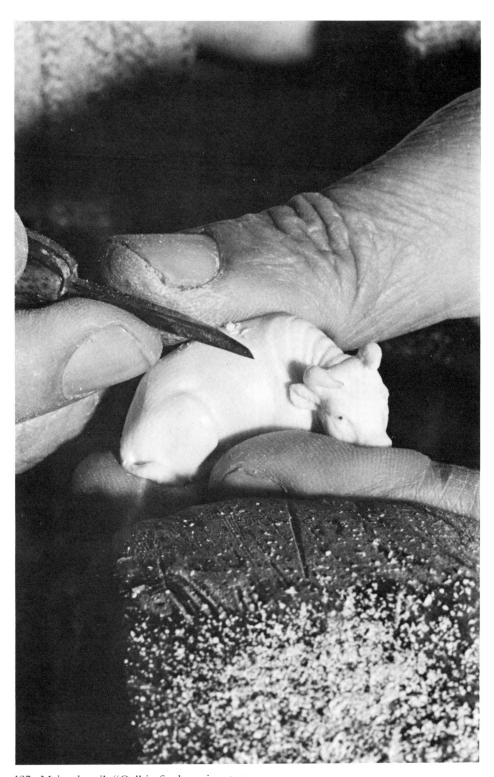

127. Meigyokusai's "Ox" in final carving stage.

Some carvers use only stain in various shades of beige and tan to dark brown —no other color. And occasionally a carver, in order to emphasize the warm luster and beautiful texture and grain of natural ivory, will make a netsuke without using either stain or paint. Some carvers, including Yoshiyuki and Masatoshi, use incense smoke instead of liquid nut stains to achieve a soft basic tint.

REVERSIBLE-FACE TECHNIQUE

The person who is just being introduced to the art of netsuke carving is particularly fascinated with the reversible face, the movable hand, a worm popping out of a chestnut, or protruding eyes. These "trick netsuke" techniques when first developed were kept secret, but today there are few secrets in the world of ivory carving.

Shogetsu was intrigued by the Kabuki dance stories in which the dancer changes masks when his back is to the audience: the fox who, in helping a man who has befriended him, turns into a woman and becomes the man's wife; the crane who becomes the wife of a mortal; and the good-and-evil opposition, often represented by Okame and Hannya. In trying to bring this transformation concept to netsuke, he developed the reversible-face technique. It has been copied by less skilled craftsmen, but difficult, intricate, and patient workmanship is always involved (Figs. 39, 40).

A cavity is first carved in the head of the figure (Fig. 128). Two (sometimes three) faces are carved on a tiny, round piece of ivory through which a hole is drilled. A minute steel bar goes through this hole and is inserted in tiny holes on each side of the head, the holes concealed by design or inlay.

In completing a netsuke that includes a reversible face, Shogetsu follows these steps: 1) After the rough form and face cavity is finished, it is polished with *tokusa* sticks and polishing powder. 2) The intricate geometric designs, which are a part of every Shogetsu netsuke, are then drawn on the ivory with a small badger-hair brush (*menso*) and etched with a fine, curved tool (Fig. 129), the artist first making sure the head fits, but not leaving it in place. 3) The form and faces are then put into the *yasha* soup (separately) and allowed to remain ten to twenty minutes (at times longer if a darker color is desired). 4) The netsuke is then carefully checked for perfection of design patterns, and portions of the netsuke that should be lighter are carefully polished. This process may

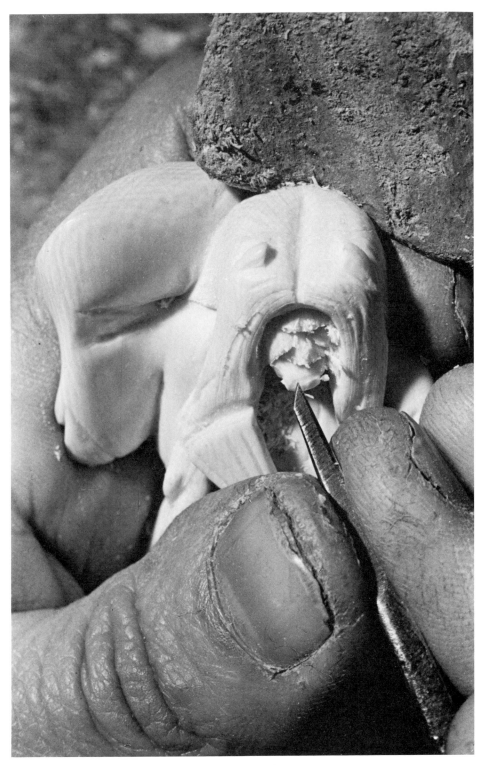

128. Shogetsu carving cavity in reversible-face technique.

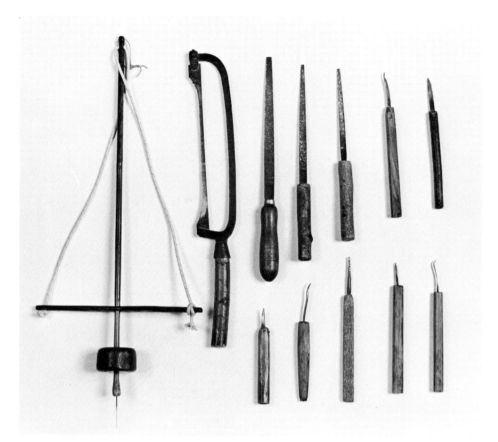

129. Tools used in reversible-face technique.

be repeated several times. 5) After the netsuke is out of the final immersion in the staining liquid, it is washed and wiped off. The reversible faces are put in place and the intricate pattern outlined with *sumi* ink, using again the small brush. 6) Finally the netsuke is lightly polished with a cloth.

Other "trick netsuke" techniques will not be described except to note that the moving-head procedure, which dates back to antique designs, involves wire, not the small rod of steel used in the reversible-face design. While most netsuke carvers have long, tapered fingers, their hands must be strong. It is difficult to understand how these strong, sometimes large hands can achieve the hair-breadth precision involved in these intricate, complicated techniques.

CHAPTER 6

A Netsuke in the Making

EACH OF the first-rank netsuke carvers has his own particular method of working out a design, of coloring and staining, of finishing and polishing. Some carvers complete one netsuke before starting another; others may have several netsuke in various stages of completion at one time. Some work from simple pencil sketches with a few guidelines drawn on the ivory; others keep beautiful Hokusai-like sketchbooks containing intricate, detailed drawings of their designs. Some make preliminary models in clay; others carve entirely from the intuitive impulses of the mind and spirit.

For all these carvers, however, skill and talent, artistic integrity, patience, and dedication are common denominators. These qualities are apparent to anyone who has watched a first-rank carver at work. The experience creates a picture that comes to mind whenever you hold a beautiful netsuke in your hand. The following photographic series, showing sixteen stages in the carving of "Puppy Chewing on a Straw Sandal," is an attempt to reproduce—to some extent—that memorable experience.

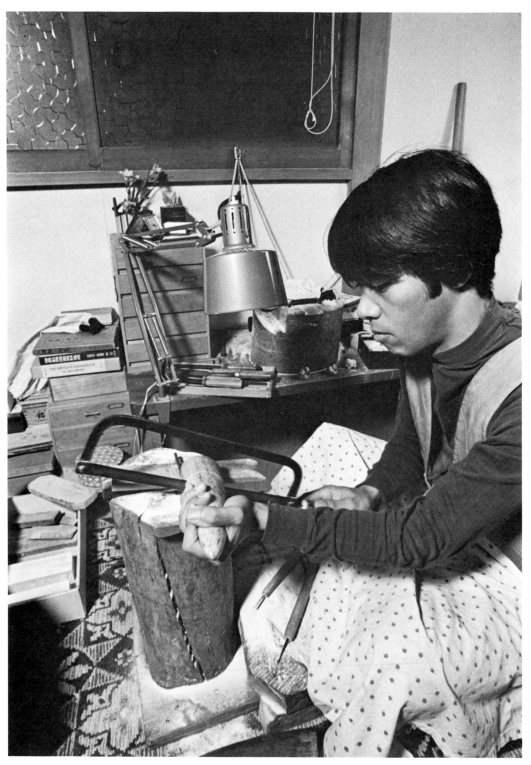

130(a). Kangyoku beginning a netsuke.

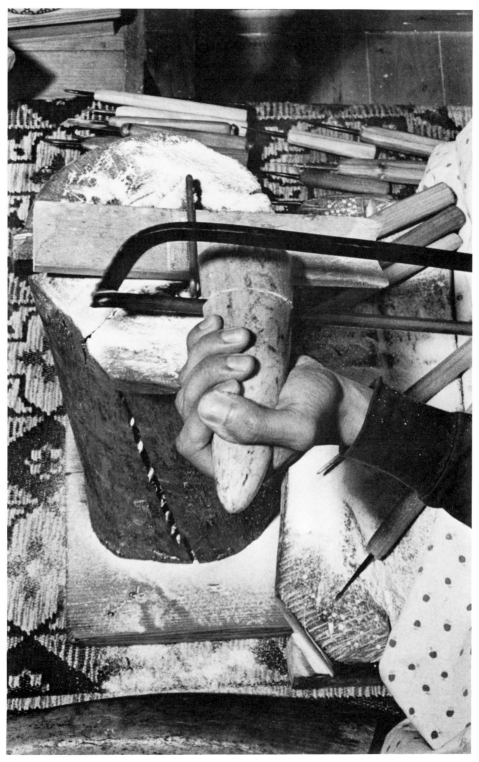

130(b). Sawing section from ivory tusk.

130(c). Ivory section with sketched guidelines.

130(d). Roughing out design shape, using saw to cut corners and edges.

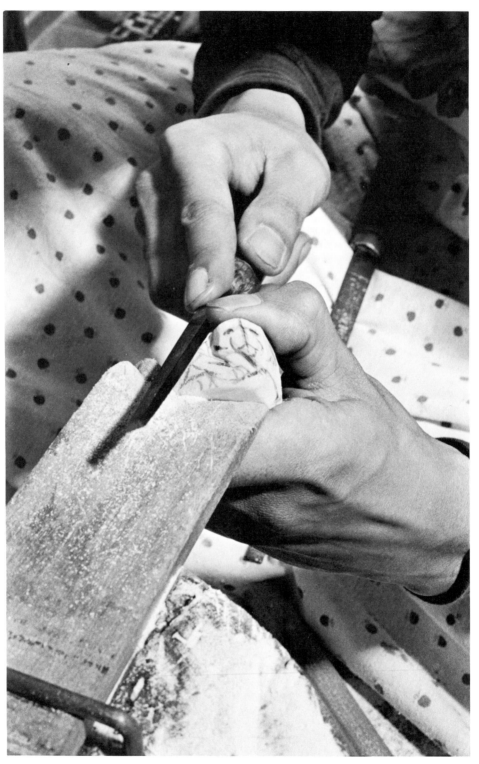

130(e). Continuing rough shaping with one-sided file (*sharime*).

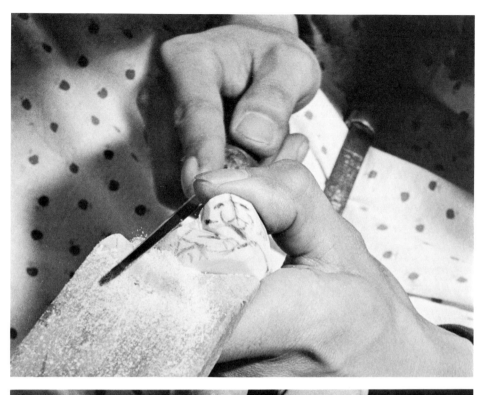

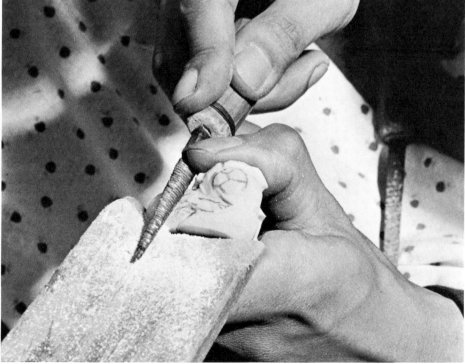

130(f, g). Further shaping with another file (*gangi*) and again with small *sharime* file.

130(h). Design emerging; note guideline drawn on surface for proper centering.

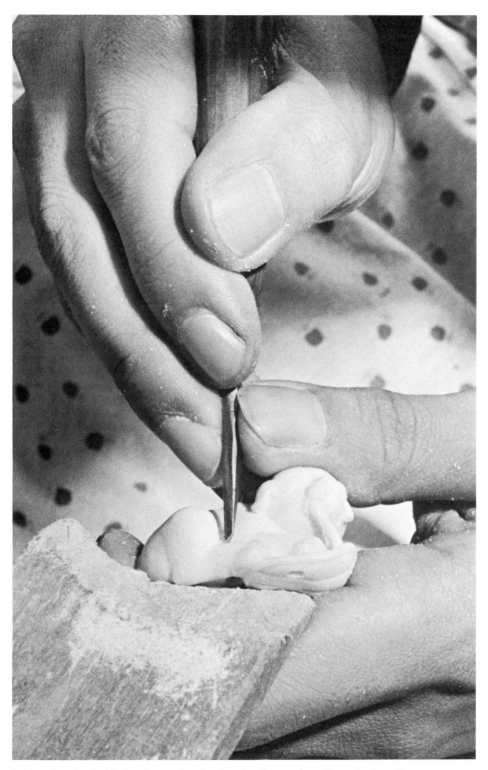

130(i). Carving knife developing details after first immersion of netsuke in stain.

130(j). Details of head and body lines begin to appear.

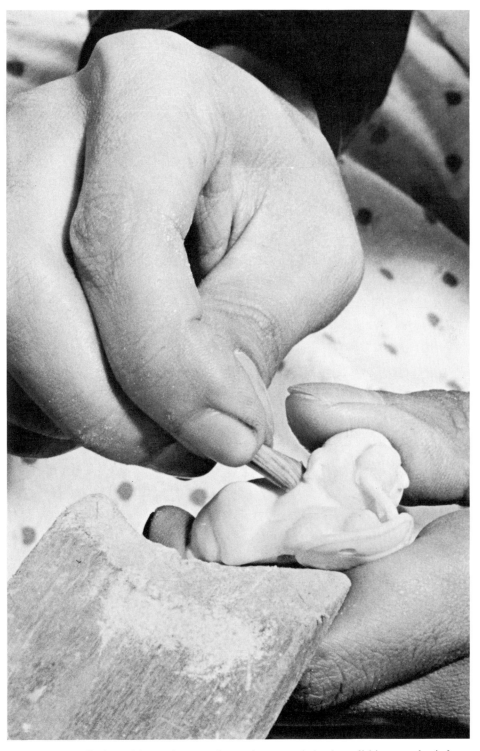

130(k). First polishing with rough stem of scouring grass (*tokusa*); polishing powder is later applied by brush.

130(1). Effect of first polishing; the staining, polishing, and carving processes will be repeated many times.

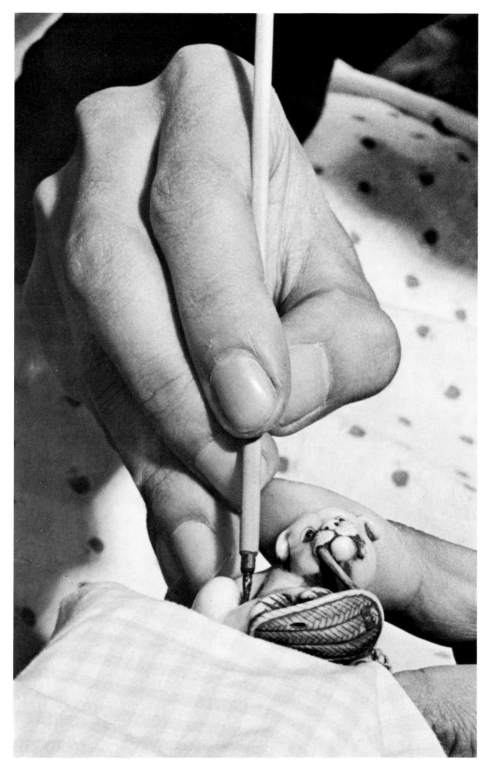

130(m). Application of *sumi*-ink hair lines and other design accents.

130(n). Effect of first *sumi*-ink detailing; ivory has darkened after repeated staining.

130(o). Last stage, after final polishing with grindstone powder (*toishi*).

130(p). Finished netsuke with tortoise-shell inlay of eyes, final *sumi*-ink application, color accents as in sandal cord, and signature (see Fig. 15).

Part Three

CHAPTER 7

Contemporary Carvers

FOR CENTURIES, the netsuke carver's world was limited. The product of his creativity was purely functional; not until the nineteenth century did it approach the status of an art form. Traditionally, the anonymity of the netsuke artist as a person was almost complete.

Today, when netsuke have been transformed from functional objects created for Japanese wearers to works of art sought by collectors throughout the world, the carver has moved closer to the collector's center of interest. This interest brings into focus the talented living artists who are responsible for the current resurgence in netsuke carving. They are sensitive, delightful human beings. Knowing them adds a new dimension to netsuke collecting.

The twenty-seven brief sketches in the following pages present a representative cross section of the leading twentieth-century carvers, a few of whom have died since this book was begun. The photographs will give the reader some idea of how contemporary netsuke carvers look and how they work. Because of limited space and time, it has been impossible, regrettably, to include in this section all of the contemporary *issaku* carvers.

The unequal space and photographic emphasis given to the different carvers are not intended to indicate their relative importance. In some instances, the availability of the artist governed the amount of material obtained. In others, the author's rapport with or her affinity for the work of a particular carver may create an emphasis that should be considered personal, not a judgment of comparative merit.

131. Bishu.

 BISHU

Bishu (or Mishu, as his signature is also read) is one of the young carvers in their thirties who have talent, imagination, and great potential. He studies antique netsuke and netsuke books, and he knows traditional netsuke forms as well as traditional techniques and workmanship criteria, but he is unfettered by them.

Bishu feels that technical perfection is not the main reason netsuke hold such fascination for so many people and have become so popular with collectors. It is rather the panorama of early Japan and its people told through the imagination and talent of the netsuke artist. Netsuke were a functional part of Japanese raiment for centuries and were created by and for the people from all walks of life. The early netsuke expressed the life, the interests, the humor, the beliefs, and the desires of the Japanese of those times. The netsuke is an art form that was a part of the life of the poor as well as the rich, the lowly as well as the mighty. No form of sculpture or other art reached so many Japanese or expressed so much of their life and culture as did the netsuke.

Today the netsuke is no longer functional and is being created chiefly for collectors, and Bishu believes that contemporary designs should reflect the free expression of the artist who is living in twentieth-century Japan. He has, for example, drawn on an old subject, the Dutchman, but his fertile imagination has created a netsuke poles apart in design from any antique carver's conception of this amusing subject (Fig. 112). Completely different in all aspects but fully as innovative is Bishu's simple, enchanting netsuke "Alighting Swan" (Fig. 13). For sheer beauty, originality, and carving skill, few twentieth-century netsuke can match it.

The freedom of expression and the carving expertise currently shown by

132. Gaho.

Bishu have created works that will no doubt summon converts to the collecting of contemporary netsuke and keep the art of netsuke carving vital for decades, perhaps centuries, to come.

Bishu (great-grandfather)—Bishu Teruichiro (grandfather)—
Shosai Saito (father)—Bishu

GAHO

A number of the great carvers of the twentieth century were born in the last decade of the nineteenth century or just after the turn of the century. Gaho (Imai) is a member of this group. His face is warm and kind; his hair is snow white, a rare characteristic among Japanese. Also seldom found in Japan is a large family like Gaho's, which has six children, ranging in age from the forties to the teens.

His carving heritage goes back to the Hakumin (Sekine) school, which he entered at fifteen. The school was founded by Hakumin, who was of samurai rank. Jitsuga, the third master of this school, was the originator of the ivory clamshell with detailed inside carvings. His pupil Gaho, the fourth master of the Hakumin school, learned all the techniques of the school, including the intricate clamshell carvings. But his own talent and skill rose above his training, and beautiful, original Gaho designs in netsuke and *okimono* soon were attracting the attention of collectors.

His lifetime of ivory carving was interrupted only by the war years, when he worked in a military factory. His best netsuke come from the prewar period and are generally smaller and more delicate than those he is producing today (Fig. 80). They are all well carved, true to netsuke tradition and techniques, and warmly accented with stain and color. His subject matter is sometimes drawn from ukiyoe prints, sometimes from genre occupations, and frequently from legend or religion. Some of his best-known netsuke subjects include *tanemaki* (the sower), the poet-priest Saigyo, and Takasago. The beautiful facial expressions of his netsuke have particular appeal for collectors, and he always depicts mores and clothing details with integrity. He carves with sensitivity and skill.

Gaho is highly regarded by collectors and carvers alike and enjoys meeting with J.I.S.A. friends. He is prominent among the older group who preserved the art of netsuke carving after its late-nineteenth-century decline and are participating in its current revival.

Hakumin—Hakujitsu—Jitsuga—Gaho

HAKURAKU

Until his death in 1974, one of the producers of first-rate netsuke was Hakuraku (Harutaro Matsuda), whose brightly tranquil face and heavy shock of black hair belied his years. Long an ivory carver, he was over sixty when he decided

133. Hakuraku.

that carving netsuke held a much greater fascination than other ivory art, and he then turned much of his creative talent in that direction.

Hakuraku's great love of beautiful ivory is evident in his netsuke. He seldom used stain and then very sparingly. Sometimes he used a touch of color for contrast but without stain, and sometimes he used no stain or color whatsoever. To the novice collector accustomed to the use of stain and color on netsuke, such a piece looks unfinished, but not to a more sophisticated buyer. The warmth and gloss of the ivory and the simplicity and strength of his designs are paramount in his netsuke. Women and children are often his subjects, but he is perhaps most famous for his sumo wrestlers. He must have had a great love and a thorough knowledge of the sport, for his wrestlers are vibrant with action and motion, and their muscular structure is depicted with honesty and realism. A student of sumo wrestling can immediately identify the throw depicted in a Hakuraku sumo netsuke (Fig. 107). Occasionally he created a highly stylized design, hard to recognize as a Hakuraku.

Many carvers work on only one netsuke at a time. New design ideas often came to Hakuraku while he was working on a netsuke. He would then stop and put it aside for the time being while he set out to follow his new creative impulse. As a result, he often had several pieces in various stages of completion at one time.

His son Michiteru worked with him. Michiteru sometimes carves netsuke but is better known for his Buddha statues. He has large shoes to fill in following his father, but, hopefully, someday he too will be one of the leading carvers of the twentieth century.

Tomochika—Masamichi—Doraku—Hakuraku—Michiteru

英
之 HIDEYUKI

134. Hideyuki.

When research on this book was begun in 1970, Hideyuki was one of the young carvers listed as "promising." By 1974 his improvement was so great that many of his pieces could unquestionably be rated as top level. Not only have his designs and carving skills in ivory shown amazing development; he has also become very versatile in techniques and materials. He is now exploring in the area of wood, lacquer, and inlay with extraordinary success. His subject matter is currently drawn from historical or legendary Japanese figures, but his netsuke are executed with his own original ideas and with delicate, detailed, and meticulous workmanship. He is also a master at carving plum-blossom and other flower netsuke. He is a great student with a dedication to his art in the finest netsuke tradition.

In 1974 Hideyuki decided to change his professional name to Kosei with a seal underneath reading Hideyuki. Kosei was the *go* of his father, from whom he learned to carve; so Hideyuki becomes Kosei II. He says Kosei means "the vast sky spreading endlessly with a hope for the future without obstruction." The name also has the same sound as the word that means "later world" or "the future." Thus Hideyuki is hoping that his netsuke with the new name will "remain in the future."

Kangyoku, Bishu, and Hideyuki are close friends, are close in age, and live in the same area near Tokyo. In a relationship reminiscent of the one between Soko Morita and Gyokuso, these three talented young carvers exchange ideas; they talk of the past, present, and future of netsuke carving; and they share with enthusiasm the rapidly changing and broadening netsuke world of today. There is no doubt that these three young men, so innovative and so gifted, will take their place in the netsuke hall of fame.

Kenko—Korin—Seiun—Kosei Sakurai—Kosei Hideyuki

芳
堂 HODO

After World War II, when Yoshio Sekizawa was very young, he graduated from a technical engineering school and went to work for a company that produced small machines. His innate ability to work with his hands and his latent creative talent soon built up so strong a desire to become an ivory carver that he left his company at nineteen and started to learn ivory carving under the great netsuke artist Hodo. While studying, he made a living carving ivory necklaces and earrings. His teacher soon realized that he had a pupil who would one day surpass his master, and he conferred on him the privilege of taking his own name as his carving signature. The master's confidence was not misplaced. The pupil in two decades has become one of the great netsuke carvers of the twentieth century.

Hodo's netsuke appeal to the amateur and sophisticated collector alike. His designs are original, and his workmanship is of the highest order. Most of his subjects are taken from everyday Japanese life—the fisherman, the sandal-maker, the sumo wrestler, the carpenter, the farmer. He carves these subjects with unassuming artistry and naturalness. Occasionally he draws from the vast fund of religious, Kabuki, and Noh-drama characters. He sometimes repeats a subject, but always it is somewhat different in design. His medium is always ivory. He employs only hand tools, self-made. He hand-polishes his netsuke, never using an electric polisher of any kind. He uses color quietly and realistically with the rough *arashi* technique—a soft, dark-brown or green jacket, a beige kimono, an occasional touch of brighter color in a basket of fruit, in an obi, or in the decoration of a kimono (Figs. 41, 104). Occasionally a Hodo netsuke will have a box containing masks, a fish basket with a removable cover containing minuscule fish, or a moving head (Figs. 102, 105). Always these details are carved with great skill and with integrity as to mores and customs—details that never dominate the quiet simplicity of the netsuke.

In examining a group of his genre figures, one thinks of the word "sculptor" rather than "carver." The expressions, the anatomy, the postures of his little figures are unbelievably lifelike. They are carved with sympathy and with humor. They are simple but powerful.

When several pieces are finished, Hodo brings them to the Sunamoto shop.

If business is quiet, he will stay and visit with Mr. Sunamoto or others in the store. He enjoys talking with them and is relaxed and good humored—a side of his personality that many never see. Occasionally he will have a game of *go* with the store manager. He likes to talk about religion, life, love, and marriage. To have a good marriage is of great concern to Hodo. His deep religious feelings are evident in his Buddha *okimono,* and his great empathy for simple, poor people finds expression in his genre netsuke. Always a student, he researches a subject with great thoroughness before starting to carve it. Hodo carves as his very honest spirit and inspiration dictate, not for money.

Hodo is serious, gentle, dedicated to the integrity of his art in the old tradition, and very much his own man. He belongs to no carving organization. He is not interested in sharing ideas about techniques, designs, or materials with his peers. He wants to create his own work in his own way. No one familiar with his work can quarrel with his philosophy.

In an effort to get away from the disturbing noises of the city, he lives on the Miura Peninsula near the sea. He likes to fish and go boating. Many years ago, he tried to make a boat by himself, but it was not well balanced. On his first excursion in it, the boat capsized, and Hodo was plunged into the sea. Undaunted, he built another boat. This time it was functional, and he finds great relaxation during the hours he spends in it.

Hodo also has achieved a name for himself as a great *okimono* carver. His Buddha statues and Noh characters are very popular with foreign collectors. He participated in the Exhibition of Ivory Carvings by Four Contemporary Artists sponsored by Mitsukoshi in 1968. Among the pieces attracting great interest were his exquisite and unusual nudes done in relief, framed for wall hanging.

Unfortunately for netsuke collectors, Hodo is now turning most of his artistic creativeness to *okimono,* and not many of his netsuke are currently reaching the market. Perhaps an increase in the knowledge and appreciation of his netsuke among collectors will bring him back to netsuke carving. That is where he belongs. He is truly a great netsuke artist.

Komei—Meido—Kodo—Hodo—Hodo

135. Hodo working on clay model.

136. Hozan.

芳
山 HOZAN

In appearance, Hozan Fujita might be an officer of a large Japanese bank. In manner and speech, he reflects the peace and quiet of the rural area where he lives. He has a proud carving lineage, starting with his father, Kando, from whom he learned to carve, and going back to the famous master Hojitsu, who in the mid-nineteenth century was considered the best carver in Tokyo and from whom the famous So school originated. Hozan's father-in-law is a wholesale ivory dealer, handling such items as chopsticks, shamisen plectrums, and chess figures. Like many carvers, Hozan writes poetry. He is also an expert calligrapher.

He chooses his netsuke subjects largely from old Japanese customs and figures. He usually carves male figures and his portrayals of Hotei, the god of happiness, are especially popular among collectors. Each Hotei is different, but all are done with warmth and humor. His genre figures, like the cormorant fisherman in Figure 103, show careful study and research of the subject as well as technical and artistic ingenuity. He uses color pleasingly to emphasize texture and design. His netsuke show originality, although dominated by tradition in basic form and subject matter. His workmanship is painstaking and detailed, and he usually spends two weeks on a single netsuke. He is very proud of having received an award from the prewar Ministry of Commerce and Industry. He is popular among fellow carvers in the J.I.S.A. and the Aisen-kai.

Hozan is a happy, warm person of many talents and tastes—and one of the best of Japan's living carvers.

Hojitsu—Hoichi—Kansai—Kando—Hozan

137. Ichio.

一
桜 ICHIO

Ichio Sakurai is a carver whose very active imagination has led him into various experimental directions, but his ultimate forte is not yet evident. His figure netsuke are sometimes quite stylized, suggestive of Ichiro's distinctive execution. In fact, I questioned a salesgirl in a Tokyo shop about a netsuke of this type. "That was carved by Ichiro's son," she replied, probably having come to this completely erroneous conclusion because of the similarity of style and name.

In an entirely different style of carving, Ichio sometimes condenses a very complicated folktale within the scope of a small netsuke. Such a story often has two or more parts, which Ichio depicts on opposite sides of a divider screen, all carved with great technical virtuosity out of a single piece of ivory.

Ichio comes from a family of creative people. His father, and teacher, is a carver; his uncle Kosei and his cousin Hideyuki are both netsuke carvers; and his sister Kazuko is a designer. Ichio himself is a Japanese-style painter as well as a carver.

Extremely versatile in technique as well as design, Ichio shows constant improvement and may eventually achieve a prominent place among twentieth-century carvers.

Korin—Seiun—Ichio

一
郎 ICHIRO

In the history of twentieth-century netsuke carving, Ichiro Inada will be re-membered particularly for his enchanting designs drawn from genre and Ka-buki subjects and as the artist who first used paint extensively on ivory. To those who have had the privilege of knowing him, he will be remembered as a warm, outgoing, dedicated artist who gives generously of himself to friends and to anyone—collector, dealer, or young carver—in his world, the netsuke world.

Threaded through his long career as a netsuke carver has always been his love of painting. At the age of twenty-five, after studying ivory carving for twelve years with the master Koichi, he was expelled for expressing the desire to study Western painting. Such an idea was heresy! But study painting Ichiro did, financing his schooling at the Nippon Bijutsuin by carving netsuke. At thirty (1921), he finished his schooling and set himself up as an ivory artist. His work during this period included *okimono* as well as netsuke, Buddhist statues, and sets of tiny animals, much smaller than netsuke, made from pieces of ivory left from *okimono* carvings.

During World War II, when ivory was virtually unobtainable, Ichiro carved netsuke from wood. Some netsuke collectors consider his wooden netsuke of this period his finest works.

After the war, when he resumed ivory carving, he concentrated mostly on figures from Kabuki plays, Japanese history, and everyday life. It was then that he felt his "little people" would be more real if he could improve meth-ods of coloring ivory. He uses pure pigments, and his blues have become an Ichiro hallmark. Other touches of color; *sumi* ink for defining hair, eyes, and eyebrows; and occasionally bits of mother-of-pearl, coral, or gold inlay com-plete his lifelike little figures. He uses only hand tools, saws, and drills. He prefers a dull finish, but what little polishing is necessary he does himself with the leaf of the *muku* tree or very fine sandpaper. His netsuke are original, carved from a rough pencil sketch; true to tradition in subject matter; strong, some-what stylized in design; and skillful but not pretentiously intricate in technique. Ichiro netsuke are unmistakably Ichiro.

His integrity in depicting the mores and the correct dress of many of his figures is illustrated in stories he tells with childlike merriment. Many years ago, when he decided to design and carve the figure of a mendicant monk, or *komuso* (Fig. 88), he went a long distance by streetcar to a Buddhist temple to borrow the headgear (usually worn down over the face) and the clothes of a *komuso* in

138. Ichiro applying color.

order to perfect his design. It was easier to wear the garments than to carry them, and on his way home he caused great glee among friends on the streetcar who teased him about changing his profession.

While still studying under Koichi, he was working on an *okimono* subject depicting an old man and a frightened little boy trying to huddle under a broken, too-small umbrella during a thunderstorm. In order to understand the feelings of the little boy, Ichiro poured water over himself. His master made him stop, with the reprimand "You're all wet and will take cold."

During his animal period, he frequently had a cat or a rabbit or a dog in the house so that he could sketch it from life before re-creating it in a piece of ivory.

Ichiro is always thinking of designs, even when drinking a cup of sakè with friends. Carving is so completely his life that if he has a day when his carving doesn't go well, he spends a sleepless night.

Personal misfortunes plagued him during much of his early life but never crushed his spirit. When he was a young boy, his father guaranteed a large loan for a friend. When the loan was defaulted, Ichiro's father had to pay it and was ruined financially. From that time on, Ichiro had to support himself, although he always received a wealth of understanding and encouragement from his father. Later, Ichiro's fiancée died before their marriage and he has remained single, making his home with his beloved adopted daughter, Nobuko. In 1946, he almost lost his life in a boardinghouse fire, and all of his models were destroyed. Now past eighty, he lives a tranquil life in his comfortable house in Tokyo, lovingly cared for by Nobuko. He still carves from sunrise to sunset, facing his little garden, interrupting his work only for visits with friends.

Unlike some carvers who lead almost monastic lives, Ichiro has many warm friends among carvers, dealers, and collectors. His closest friend for many years was Shigeo Tsujita, who became his business agent in 1961. In the fall of 1971, the seventy-seven-year-old Tsujita died. His family wanted an Ichiro netsuke buried with him "to keep him company." To comply with the family's request, Ichiro carved the figure of Ryokan, a saintly Buddhist priest who loved children. Ichiro himself always wanted to be like Ryokan and chose this subject for the wooden netsuke to be buried with his dear friend.

Ichiro, a gentle, dignified, talented man, has brought much joy to netsuke collectors and has contributed toward keeping alive the art of netsuke carving.

Hojitsu—Hoichi—Koichi—Ichiro

139. Kangyoku.

寛玉 KANGYOKU

Kangyoku (Noriyoshi Tachihara) is the youngest of Japan's living first-rank netsuke artist-carvers. He is at once centuries old in his use of basic netsuke forms, techniques, and subjects and as modern as tomorrow in many of his designs. He links the past not only with the present but also with the future. He is one of the young carvers who are beginning to break the old design molds and are striking out in new directions. Some of them are still searching. Their almost radical ideas haven't quite jelled. Kangyoku in his innovative designs seems very sure of himself. He sometimes carves with tongue in cheek but to delight and amuse the viewer, not to fool him.

Surprisingly, when I showed Kangyoku's abstract rabbit and *shishi* (Figs. 26, 27) to two friends who have superior collections of antique netsuke, I did not offend their purist taste. Instead, they were fascinated and impressed. Both expressed their intention of adding some contemporary netsuke to their collections and spoke of their preference for completely new and original designs rather than remakes of traditional versions.

Kangyoku is a handsome young man with large, inquisitive eyes and a face that, in repose, is serious and almost brooding. When he smiles, which he does often, his broad, infectious grin lights up his whole face, and he becomes a different person. Great warmth comes through his apparent shyness, and quickly he seems like an old friend in spite of the language barrier.

Kangyoku's attractive personality is comprised of many qualities: his talent, his youth, his modesty, his generosity, his discipline, and his dedication. An example of his modest generosity was evidenced during the preparation of this book. One day at luncheon at the Palace Hotel, Mr. Sugimura and I agreed that Kangyoku should be featured in the chapter on the making of a netsuke, not only because of his basic talent and photogenic good looks but also because his youth would serve to emphasize that netsuke carving is by no means a dead or dying art. Kangyoku modestly agreed to the arrangement, and Michi and Mr. Sugimura proceeded to discuss with him a mutually convenient time for the photography session. Two days later, Michi received a soul-rending letter from Kangyoku. After further consideration, he felt that he must decline the assignment. An older, more deserving artist should be selected, he said. From the tone of the letter, it was obvious that it was a decision Kangyoku felt compelled to make, but he did so reluctantly. Much persuasion was required before he changed his mind and agreed to continue with the original arrangement.

To illustrate Kangyoku's kindness and empathic nature, his wife Naomi tells of an incident during their courtship when he was taking her home late on a very cold, frosty night. On the way, they met an old woman from the country who was frightened and lost. Kangyoku ascertained the address of the place she was trying to find and insisted upon taking her to the home of her friends some distance away before continuing to Naomi's home.

Naomi is a beautiful, intelligent girl with a great love for Kangyoku and his art. She understands the carver's need of serene working conditions and makes every effort to provide the proper environment so that he can achieve his great goal: to become as good as some of the greatest of antique carvers.

By nature, Kangyoku is tense and nervous. After carving eight hours a day, five days a week, he relaxes for two days. He enjoys playing golf and is interested in spectator sports. Reading, studying, hiking, and playing with his baby daughter fill the rest of his leisure days.

He learned to carve from his father, the second Kangyoku (Fusakichi), who belonged to the Hojitsu school and was famous for his animal *okimono*. Kangyoku, too, has a great love for animals but has always been more interested in netsuke than in *okimono*. At fifteen he carved his first netsuke, a little tiger. Subsequently, he graduated from Saitama University with a major in economics. At this crossroads of his life, he had to make a choice: netsuke carver or businessman. The force of his latent talent and his love of carving and the creative life it offered won the decision, and the world of netsuke is the richer for it. Before he was twenty-five, he was firmly established as one of Japan's most promising ivory netsuke carvers, especially in the field of animal subjects.

Although Kangyoku has probably done more experimenting in abstract and surrealist designs than any other contemporary netsuke artist, he adheres meticulously to traditional carving techniques. His designs are bold and strong, with gentle exaggerations, or "deformations," as he calls them. His netsuke all have pleasing tactile qualities, and he conforms to the old basic netsuke shapes and forms (Figs. 8, 9, 14).

For discipline and training, carvers of antique netsuke as well as contemporary carvers began their carving careers by copying designs of their master or other members of their "school," or by using old, classic netsuke designs. As their techniques improved, their own originality became increasingly apparent. Kangyoku is no exception. The origin of many of his design ideas can be traced to early netsuke, but his netsuke are always readily recognized as coming from the distinctive hands of Kangyoku.

During the National Athletic Meet in 1967, the Empress of Japan visited Saitama Prefecture, where Kangyoku lives. There she saw some of his netsuke on display. She was delighted with his "jewel" rabbit and promptly bought it. A similarly designed rabbit netsuke by Kangyoku, dating from 1970, is shown in Figure 11.

In his early thirties, Kangyoku is one of Japan's most popular contemporary netsuke carvers. If, in the next decade or two, his creativeness and his skill continue to develop as in the past decade, he could well become one of the great netsuke carvers of all time.

Hojitsu—Hoitsu—Kansai—Kanji—Kangyoku—Kangyoku—Kangyoku

(Kangyoku I died at twenty-one and was succeeded by his brother, Kangyoku II, who was succeeded by his son Kangyoku III.)

桂
雲 KEIUN

Every morning between five and eight o'clock, Minosuke Ohmura, known to the netsuke world as Keiun, can be found fishing on the banks of the Uji River, which runs past the Byodo-in, one of Japan's most famous and most beautiful temples. He not only likes to fish, but he also likes to cook the fish he catches. In fact, he refuses to eat fish cooked by anyone else.

The Ohmura home near the famous Uji tea fields tells much about Keiun's life, his tastes, and his character. Keiun has a pretty wife, Tamiko, who is a companion with the intuition not to distract her artist-husband. In her, he has found a guardian of his regulated and creative life. Keiun cannot stand disorder. It distresses and upsets him, and Tamiko keeps the house spotlessly clean and neat. He likes to play *go* and occasionally performs the tea ceremony. He likes music, particularly the piano. He is a religious man and belongs to a sect founded by the Buddhist priest Nichiren. On first meeting, he is reserved and very serious. Actually, he has a warm sense of humor and likes to tease and joke with his wife and with friends. A fluffy white dog named Mary, with a pink ribbon in her hair, rules the household. Keiun and Tamiko like to travel but are unable to do so now, since they will not leave Mary.

Keiun started to learn carving at eighteen under the *okimono* artist Tsuji. But the statues of beautiful T'ang-dynasty women that he was carving under Tsuji did not strike a responsive artistic chord in Keiun. After three years, he left his master to find an outlet for his talent in a field more meaningful to him and more representative of Japan's true artistry. Netsuke carving seemed to be his answer, and he studied very hard by himself, haunted museums, and examined antique netsuke at every opportunity. He was especially influenced by Kaigyokusai. A fusion of inherent talent and skill, together with determination and industry, has produced in Keiun one of the great netsuke carvers of the twentieth century.

His animals are simple and have great tactile appeal. In late years, however, some of his more detailed designs have become so popular that currently he produces few animals. He is best known for his "Cleaning the Buddha" subject which depicts the annual cleaning of the 53.5-foot Nara Daibutsu (Fig. 117). A tour de force it is—complete with diminutive ladders, buckets, ropes, and thirty-three human figures—yet its overall composition conveys primarily the

140. Keiun working on a netsuke.

beauty and serenity of the Buddha. All collectors of Keiun netsuke want this subject, and he has repeated it, with variations, a number of times. Other favorite Keiun subjects are drawn from Japanese and Chinese folklore—for example, "The Nightingale and the Plum Tree" (Fig. 47), "Rosei's Dream" (Fig. 55), and "Kume no Sennin" (Fig. 56). These stories are depicted with imagination and detailed, intricate refinement. Keiun's dedication to technical perfection, however, never becomes fussy or busy. When a Keiun netsuke is examined carefully, it is easy to understand why he spends two weeks on a single piece.

Keiun has carved for Kohachiro Yokoyama of Kyoto for more than thirty years. Through the Yokoyama shops in Tokyo and Kyoto, as well as through export, Keiun netsuke have found their way into the hands of collectors of contemporary netsuke throughout the world. Many collectors of antique netsuke include Keiun netsuke in their collections because in his work they recognize skill and talent fully comparable to those of the old netsuke masters.

 KOYU

Koyu (Kazuo Tanaka) is one of the five carvers who are responsible for the formation of the J.I.S.A. He is a serious student of netsuke techniques and design and is a fine carver, dedicated to doing everything possible to keep the art alive. As a founder of J.I.S.A., he is very active in its programs and plans. He firmly believes that such cooperative effort can provide not only ideas and inspiration but also the practical assistance that is equally important in encouraging talented young men to resist the financial enticement of Japan's present industrial world in favor of becoming a part of the netsuke world.

Since netsuke art developed and flourished in earlier centuries, Koyu believes the life and customs of those days should provide the subject ideas of his netsuke: a famous old samurai, Okubo Hikozaemon (Fig. 87); a man trying to learn *go* by himself (Fig. 98); and a reformed Tanuki (p. 85). His figures are usually male and always realistic; his designs are original and give great attention to the hair and dress styles of the period. He is very proficient in the use of color

141. Koyu engrossed in his work.

142. Koyu's netsuke taking shape (see Fig. 87).

and stain to emphasize textures and delineate design and form. He uses the *arashi* technique in applying color and rarely uses color other than shades of brown.

New designs are constantly running through Koyu's mind. When one forms, he makes a simple sketch on paper, sometimes rendering the design in clay before starting to work in ivory. He spends a week to fifteen days on a netsuke, and the longer he works on a piece, the better it is, he says. However, he finds that the more he carves, the more difficult it is. Perhaps that is a sign of increasing perfectionism.

Koyu was in military service during the war. He did not start to carve until about 1950, when he began to study under Shiko Hori, whose carving lineage goes back to Tomochika (1800–1873), the great carver-teacher. He has won awards at ivory-carving exhibitions and from the Japan Art Association. He works in a neat, efficient, well-lighted studio and leads a well-ordered life with his wife and a teen-age son and daughter. His recreation hours are filled with activities from both old and new Japan: theater and movies, bowling and playing *go,* visiting exhibitions and museums, and traveling.

Koyu, like most of the contemporary carvers, is hard-working and energetic. He gives of his talent to increase the pleasure of netsuke collectors throughout the world, and he gives of himself to fellow carvers to help perpetuate the art.

Tomochika—Tomotoshi—Masamichi—Shiko—Koyu

MASATOSHI

Masatoshi is a descendant of twenty-two generations of Buddhist-image carvers. Born Tokisada Nakamura, Masatoshi started to learn carving at eighteen from his father, Kuya. Long famous for his *okimono,* most of which were based on Buddhist subjects, Kuya did not start to carve netsuke until he was forty. In netsuke annals he certainly will be listed as one of the great carvers of the early part of the twentieth century, although some netsuke purists might feel his netsuke are too intricate and delicate to meet the functional requirements of antique netsuke (Fig. 120).

Masatoshi is not as well known to collectors as his work merits. For close to twenty years, his entire output has been taken by Raymond Bushell, and very few netsuke with the Masatoshi signature (or Tokisada, a *go* he sometimes uses) reach the marketplace today. He leads a quiet life with his wife, his daughter, her stockbroker husband, and their little boy and girl, to whom Masatoshi is devoted. He carves only at night when the family is asleep and the world quiet.

A somewhat nervous person, Masatoshi has the complete, all-consuming dedication to his art that for centuries has marked the great netsuke artists. There is always a twinkle in his eye, however, and his inherent sense of fun and humor finds expression in many of his netsuke. I related to him an anecdote about his father that a carver had told me. Kuya, according to the story, kept his eyes in good condition by drinking *mamushi-zake,* which is produced by putting a live, red snake (*mamushi*) into a bottle of very strong sakè and letting it stand for a year. I asked Masatoshi if this were true and if he used the same remedy. He smiled and said that the story about his father was true. He said he, too, drank *mamushi-zake,* but he put the snake in whiskey.

Taking pictures is Masatoshi's chief hobby, and he keeps a photographic record of all his netsuke. In looking through his album, one is struck with his boundless imagination and versatility. In some of his netsuke, the Kuya influence is strongly evident (Fig. 34). However, Masatoshi's creative mind brings forth original designs, which he seldom repeats, covering almost any Japanese subject—from realistic to fanciful animals, from Buddhist to Kabuki characters, from legendary to genre figures, from amusing abstractions to wild grotesqueries.

His choice of materials is equally varied: wood of many kinds, whale tooth, hippopotamus tusk, tortoise shell, and his favorite and most frequent medium,

143. Masatoshi. Photo by Raymond Bushell.

ivory. His designs are worked out mentally and brought to life with his skilled fingers without any clay models or penciled sketches to guide him. He sometimes carves with great simplicity and quietness, sometimes with infinite detail and remarkable facial expressions. He says he prefers the old traditional form to the netsuke that are more nearly miniature *okimono*, because he finds it easier to carve humorous subjects in the traditional form. He spends up to 175 hours on his better netsuke and usually works seven nights a week. Occasionally he will relax for two or three days, when he sometimes visits bookstores or takes his grandchildren and his camera to the park.

He uses stain and color very sparingly, but engraved, decorative patterns and skillful technique in simulating fur or hair are often marks of a Masatoshi netsuke (Fig. 34). When he stains his Kabuki and man figures, he treats the ivory with the *yasha* "soup" used by most ivory carvers, but he uses incense smoke when finishing his animals and other netsuke subjects. For this purpose, he uses ordinary incense and places the netsuke over the holes of the burner in such a position that the smoke can envelop it. The length of time it is left over the smoke depends on the quality of the ivory. Sometimes thirty minutes is long enough for the first coloration. The netsuke is then polished and smoked repeatedly until the desired color is obtained. After the last polish, if there is any unevenness or sticky residue, it is wiped off with alcohol and then rubbed with a cloth to achieve the final shiny, soft finish.

His extraordinary versatility sometimes defies immediate recognition, but close examination of the incomparable workmanship will invariably bring identification of a Masatoshi netsuke. By any standard, Masatoshi is one of the great netsuke carvers of all time.

Shingyoku—Kuya—Masatoshi

明
玉
斉 MEIGYOKUSAI

To the netsuke collector, the name of Meigyokusai (or Meigin, the professional carving name he used until he was seventy) is synonymous with expert workmanship, strong and usually traditional design, and great versatility. To the Japanese interested in poetry, he is Koju Hiraga (or Koju, his pen name), famous for his five published books of *senryu* (short, earthy or humorous poems similar to haiku). In the 50,000 *senryu* he has written since 1919 (when he was twenty-three) he has described the lives of his people, including a series depicting the confusion, misery, and low morale existing at the end of World War II.

On his sixtieth birthday, Meigyokusai's *senryu* pupils erected a monument in his honor at the Tensho-ji temple in Kyoto—the first time such recognition had been given a living *senryu* poet. In rough translation, the Meigyokusai poem carved on the monument reads as follows: "When the lights come on, Kyoto is like a *go* board and is indeed the capital of the world." The simile springs from the fact that a map or an aerial photo of Kyoto's straight streets and symmetrical blocks resembles the board for the Japanese game of *go*.

We went to see Meigyokusai at his home in Kyoto. After removing our shoes, we carefully climbed the steep, narrow-treaded stairs. As we stepped into his studio, the overall impression of the room was orderliness with a catholicity of interests: cabinets of small treasures collected over a lifetime; books of poetry, history, and many books on netsuke, both in English and Japanese; a small skull *okimono*, fantastically carved; and the constant chattering of parakeets in the background. Dominating the room was Meigyokusai sitting on a cushion on the tatami floor in front of a low table on which countless carving tools were laid out with great precision. His face is unlined and expressive, and he talks with great enthusiasm. He loves to tell the story of the skull. His master's master, Gyokuzan, carved two very famous skulls, one of which was exhibited at the 1909 World Exposition in Paris and is now on exhibit in the Kyoto National Museum. The second one is in the Tokyo National Museum. After his death, Meigyokusai secured from his widow the real skull that Gyokuzan had used as his model, and, using it in turn, he carved the skull that has a place of honor in his studio. He worked on it for months, and when it was finished, he took ten days of rest, a most unusual indulgence for a carver. Many collectors, especially doctors, have wanted to buy it, but Meigyokusai adamantly refuses. He is certain that someday it will be named a "national treasure."

In this room, poetry and carving mix freely, with talent and creativity abundantly expended on both art forms.

With his pen, Meigyokusai describes in poetry the lives of his contemporaries. With his carver's tools, he brings to life in netsuke the tales and the customs of his people from an earlier era. While most of his netsuke are legendary figures or his own versions of classical designs, he also likes to carve animals, sometimes combining all the zodiac animals in a single netsuke. In the hands of a less skilled craftsman or less talented artist, this type of design could be busy or a mere tour de force. In Meigyokusai's hands, it becomes a beautifully designed netsuke of the highest order, magnificently executed (Fig. 7). He sometimes carves from rough sketches and occasionally, as in the case of the zodiac netsuke, will pencil a few lines on the ivory. Usually, however, he carves only from a design sharply etched in his mind.

Meigyokusai is one of the few first-rank contemporary carvers privileged to have a son interested in carving—a son to whom he can give the benefit of his talent and the training and skill that came from his masters: Shogin, Shozan, and Gyokuzan. Tanetoshi, like his father, is also a poet and already has nearly 15,000 published *senryu* to his credit. His favorite netsuke subjects are animals, done from sketches made at the zoo, and Chinese children's stories. He often visits the zoo and museums, following his father's advice: "More can be learned from what one sees than from what one reads." He is devoted to his father and with daily exposure to his skill and warmth of spirit, Tanetoshi will probably reach his goal of becoming a great netsuke carver.

Meigyokusai's interest in carrying on the artistic traditions of Japan extends beyond teaching his son. He has between fifty and sixty pupils in *senryu,* and once a month he travels to one of the larger cities of Japan to lecture on the art of writing *senryu* poetry.

He is deeply religious, and he says that when he carves a Buddhist statue he breathes his soul into it, or else he could never finish it. But he adds that before the statue is sold, the dealer asks a Buddhist priest to take his soul out; otherwise, the dealer would be cursed.

For decades, virtually all of Meigyokusai's carvings were handled by Mr. H. Nakayama, Sr., one of Japan's most respected dealers. Their relationship went far beyond that of agent and artist. They were the closest of friends. When Mr. Nakayama retired and closed his Kyoto store in 1967, his son, Hirokazu, manager of their Tokyo store, wanted his father and mother to come to Tokyo

144. Meigyokusai at his workbench.

145. Meigyokusai in his workroom; Tanetoshi, the artist's son, in foreground.

to live. His father quietly but flatly refused, saying, "If I move to Tokyo, I can't see my friend Meigyokusai every day." He then built his retirement home in the Momoyama district of Kyoto, where he could remain close to his lifelong friend.

Artist-carver, poet, teacher, lecturer, family man, friend, Meigyokusai is a serious but warmhearted man of many interests and many talents. Most of all, he is a man who is adding a proud page to the history of twentieth-century netsuke carving.

Gyokuzan—Shozan—Shogin—Meigyokusai (Meigin)

146. Ryoshu.

艮
舟 RYOSHU

Shozo Miyazawa grew up in a creative atmosphere because his father was the very fine netsuke carver Ryoshu. But young Shozo found his artistic outlet in painting. Then came World War II, and he spent seven years in military service. At thirty, when he returned to civilian life, he decided to become a carver. His father gave him instructions as well as his carving name.

Ryoshu studies constantly and is an indefatigable worker. He has to be. Unlike most carvers who have only one or two children, Ryoshu has a family of eight. In Japan today, the task of feeding and clothing a wife and eight children is an almost insurmountable one, especially with the limited income potential of an ivory carver. His oldest son is now carving with him, and his second son is at Tokyo University of Arts, majoring in carving. Apparently the boys have inherited Ryoshu's talent and love of carving and are undaunted by the economic limitations of such a profession.

Ryoshu is a carver's carver and is extremely well liked among fellow J.I.S.A. members. He is active in the organization and served as its first president from 1965 and 1969. In 1972 he was again elected president.

Among collectors, Ryoshu is perhaps best known for his Daruma and enchanting *kappa* netsuke: a *kappa* catching an eel through a lily pad (Fig. 29) or a *kappa* Indian-wrestling with a frog. These netsuke are designed with humor and originality and skillfully executed, using the *ukashibori* technique (designs standing out in relief). Now Ryoshu is endeavoring to break away from his *kappa* image and is experimenting in new design fields, including fish and animal abstracts, some of which are very good (Fig. 19).

Ryoshu believes that the designing and carving of netsuke offer an artist unending challenge and satisfaction. Carving is his vocation and his avocation. It is his hobby and his joy.

Tomochika—Yasuchika—Yuraku—Munetoshi—Munemasa—Ryoshu—Ryoshu

189

RYUSHI

To the person knowledgeable in the world of contemporary netsuke, the name Ryushi conjures up opulent court scenes from *The Tale of Genji* and little ivory figures reminiscent of the Heian age, some of them true to traditional netsuke form, some miniature *okimono,* and all elegant, serene, and beautiful.

Ryushi comes from a famous carving family. He learned to carve from his father Ryusui, whose lineage goes back to the Shungetsu school. His uncle was the carver Yoko, who died in 1974 and for whom he had great respect and affection. His grandfather, Ryusai, was a famous carver and teacher, and his brother, Ryuho, is a fine *okimono* carver. Ryushi first made his living by doing finish carving (*shiage*) but used every spare moment to study and learn to be an *issaku* netsuke carver.[1] His subjects are generally drawn from the world of women: babies, little girls, *maiko,* and geisha, and, particularly, elegant court ladies from the gay, luxurious Heian period. His wife is beautiful, and friends can usually recognize her lovely face in his exquisite feminine figures.

The workmanship of a Ryushi netsuke is delicate and detailed, and the finish, polish, and coloring are exceptional. Ryushi uses color sparingly but with originality. He produces his own colors—twenty of them—from a lacquer-paint base. Natural components are added for various shades. By adding the metallic element titanium he achieves the warm, rosy rust shade that has become almost a Ryushi hallmark. He has found that dissolving the colors in a starchy paste preserves the color life on the ivory. After completing the carving, he polishes the netsuke. Then he colors and stains it, and finally polishes it again. On a figure in formal kimono, he achieves the heaviness of brocade, the smoothness of silk, and the softness of flesh.

Some netsuke artists strive primarily for perfection in technique; some for the capturing of the story through their creative impulses. Some are influenced by what the buyer wants—to the subjugation of their own artistry. A combination of motivations can be found in the work of most of the living carvers. The story and the technique are all-important to Ryushi. He is adamant against the ideas of older carvers concerning what constitutes a real netsuke, just as he is against most dealer and buyer suggestions. He carves in his own way, regardless of potential salability. He wants above all to be a great artist and bring new ideas into the netsuke world.

The first time my husband and I met Ryushi, Hodo and Shodo were also

147. Ryushi carving a netsuke.

present. It was the first time these three great carvers had been together, and they promptly engaged in a heated and animated discussion concerning several netsuke questions, particularly that of "functional" versus "nonfunctional" netsuke designs. Ryushi firmly believes this generation and coming generations of netsuke collectors will accept new and completely different designs even though they are more miniature *okimono* than traditional netsuke. Whether his theory is right or whether it is because of the quiet beauty and the superb workmanship of his tiny sculptures, his work is eagerly sought by discerning collectors who are willing to pay top prices for it.

He is a perfectionist. If his carving fails to please him or he makes even a small mistake, he starts over again—and again. Usually, when working on a new design, he starts over at least three times. He spends seven to ten days on each netsuke and almost as much time in creating a new design.

Ryushi is a man of contradictions. He likes a joke, and his whimsical humor can be seen in his "Dreaming Hotei" (Fig. 59). Generally, however, he takes the world and the people in it very seriously. Almost all Ryushi netsuke have a quiet quality—serene and relaxed. In life, Ryushi has a passion for everything that moves: automobiles and airplanes, toy cars and trains. He always wanted an automobile and in 1971 was able to realize his life's ambition. After driving his new car two or three days, he proudly took his carver friend Seigyoku for a ride. The ride ended abruptly with a traffic accident. Fortunately, neither was seriously hurt, the car was repaired, and is often used on Ryushi's day off, since traveling is his favorite and most relaxing hobby.

When Ryushi first brought some netsuke to the Sunamoto shop in 1961, they were taken mostly from older designs and were not great netsuke. Mr. Sunamoto could see his potential, however, and encouraged him to work on original designs. He studied and worked very hard and has now developed a style so completely his own that it is never necessary to look at the signature to identify a Ryushi netsuke. In his early forties, he has decades in which to add beauty and joy to the world of netsuke collecting.

Shungetsu—Ryusai—Ryusui—Ryushi

生
玉 SEIGYOKU

148. Seigyoku.

Artists are born with talent. What they do with that talent depends on their strength of character, their patience and industry, their desire to learn and to explore new avenues of expression, their artistic integrity, and their economic ability to retain that integrity. Some artists take the middle road. They only nibble at the fringe of their artistic potential. On the other hand, they seldom do poor work. Other artists, with great perfectionism, create some masterpieces. They are unhappy with anything less. As a result, there can be considerable spread in the quality of their work. Seigyoku is such an artist.

Born Nobuo Kaneko, Seigyoku was trained under the netsuke artist Dosei Takeuchi. His designs are original and good; his techniques and workmanship of high order. He is one of the contemporary carvers recognized and sought by collectors. His subjects are usually figures from Japanese history and literature (Figs. 85, 122). He uses stain but not much color. Sometimes he prefers to leave the ivory in its natural state.

Seigyoku remains in the artistic world in his avocations—music, painting, and writing poetry. True to inherent Japanese sensitivity to the harmony between art and nature, he spends his leisure hours in gardening, fishing, walking in the woods, and painting.

Seigyoku spends three weeks on his best netsuke. And some of his best netsuke are almost masterpieces. Sometimes, however, his perfectionism and theoretical approach stifle his artistic creativeness, and the resulting netsuke is not great. He is always dissatisfied with his lesser netsuke, recognizing with honesty the disparity of quality. This is good. When the quality of more of his netsuke shows his real potential, Seigyoku will unquestionably be ranked among the first-rate carvers of the twentieth century.

149. Shinryo.

親眼 SHINRYO

Shinryo (Suzuki) is a many-faceted artist who started his carving education at fourteen under the master Tomioka, famous for his relief carving. After eleven years, Shinryo became independent of his first master and in 1938 started to study the technique of solid carving under Shinsho (Kikuchi), one of this century's foremost carvers. Always original and unique in his designs and techniques, Shinryo has received many awards over the years, and his works find favor with a wide range of collectors.

His versatility extends from large tusk relief carvings to *okimono* to netsuke. His choice of subjects runs the gamut from Buddhist figures to the Virgin Mary; from legendary and historical characters of old Japan to genre figures of today; from realistic dogs, tigers, and monkeys to highly stylized roosters and hens (Fig. 12). His workmanship and techniques are skilled, and his designs may be quietly simple or extremely detailed. Always he has the capacity to bring warmth from the ivory.

Like most extremely talented artists, Shinryo constantly looks for new channels of expression. A lifetime dream of his has been to carve a mural on a large plane of ivory in bas-relief. Netsuke collectors hope that in the future he will direct more of his time and artistic creativeness toward netsuke production because it is an art form in which Shinryo truly has great potential.

Komei—Shimmei—Shinsho—Shinryo

SHINSHO

Shinsho, whose actual name was Yasugoro Kikuchi, was a representative member of the Ivory Carving Association of Japan after the war in 1945. One of the outstanding descendants of the Komei school, he was an excellent teacher as well as a carver, and many of his pupils are well known in the world of ivory carving today. They include Shimmitsu (or Shinko), Shindo, Shinryo, Shinzan, and Shingetsu.

Shinsho's specialty was human figures, and he carved only in ivory. His subjects were often taken from poetry and were elegant and beautiful. Many of the early collectors of contemporary netsuke became Shinsho fans and eagerly looked for his work.

Even after he was past eighty, he worked from nine in the morning to five in the afternoon every day until shortly before his death.

As a man, as an artist, and as a teacher, Shinsho has a proud place in twentieth-century netsuke carving.

Komei (Ishikawa)—Chikaaki (Sato)—Shinsho (Kikuchi)

SHINZAN MASANAO

Among the first-rank twentieth-century carvers currently producing netsuke, Shinzan Masanao is the only one who works exclusively in wood. Since he is the last of the Masanao carvers, many of his subjects are from the original Masanao sketchbook, which belongs to him, and his workmanship is quite comparable to that of the early, distinguished Masanaos.

As a very young man, he divided his talent and interest between woodcarving and painting. His father, Masakiyo, was a great carver, and Shinzan grew up in a home dominated by the dedication that characterizes the netsuke artist. Shinzan, who was born Yoshio Sakai in 1904, was fascinated by the

150. Shinzan Masanao.

challenge of working on intricate things and decided upon netsuke carving as his profession. Under his father's training, he started carving at eighteen. Some great artist once said, "If the pupil does not surpass the master, he has failed." Shinzan did not fail. He has become one of the great carvers of the twentieth century.

In a small town in Mie Prefecture on the Ise Peninsula, Shinzan lives a quiet life. He usually spends three to four weeks on his better netsuke and works seven days a week without a definite rest day. Between netsuke, he relaxes by taking long walks and working in his garden. He usually uses boxwood (*tsuge*), and occasionally wood from the olive tree. His favorite subjects are animals (Figs. 6 and 18), but some of his most intricate and outstanding work is based on legends and folktales (Fig. 58). He does painstaking and beautiful work in the old netsuke tradition.

Several years ago, when asked if he had received awards for his carving, he replied that he did not allow himself to be exposed to the "outside." He said some carvers who had been honored for excellent work had become conceited, and, as a consequence, their work had suffered. More recently, however, through the interest of contemporary netsuke collectors in his fine work, he has been exposed to the "outside" and is receiving merited attention and recognition. And he has found that recognition can have its rewards. Just as meeting a carver adds a new dimension to netsuke collecting, so meeting collectors has added a new dimension to the life of Shinzan and his wife. They are now doing some traveling and have added a number of collectors, as well as carvers and dealers, to their circle of friends. Carving, however, is still his life, and with the money he now receives he can take the time to produce great netsuke.

Many years ago, a war injury impaired Shinzan's hearing. His devoted wife remains constantly at his side when others are present so that he won't miss any of the conversation. They are warm, hospitable people who quickly seem like old friends in spite of the language barrier. During a delightful evening at their home, Shinzan's sense of humor was evident when it was pointed out to him that the little ivory worm didn't come out of a chestnut he had carved. With a twinkle in his eye, he said, "He likes it so well in there, he doesn't want to come out."

Raising four daughters on the precarious and meager income of a netsuke carver was not easy. Today, with successful sons-in-law and higher netsuke prices, life is easier for the Sakai family. The husband of Shinzan's oldest daughter, whom he has adopted and who bears his name, is learning to carve, and one of his daughters is also testing her talent under her father's tutelage. If one of them becomes a great netsuke carver, the Masanao tradition will be kept alive.

Masanao I—Masakatsu—Masakiyo—Shinzan Masanao

SHODO

As a teen-ager, Hiroshi Asaoka learned to carve ivory figures and plants in the Shomin school, while the master Shoun Kobayashi urged him to try wood-carvings and India-ink drawings. In June of 1942, Shomin conferred on him the *go* of Shodo. As World War II intensified, he was forced to discontinue his study, and he entered military service as an airman.

Like many young men of his generation, Shodo returned from his war years to find his parents in the depths of poverty. He took a job as a cook's apprentice at the Tokyo Kaikan to support them. He learned French cooking so well that before long he was making enough money to marry.

One day, on his way to the restaurant where he worked, he saw a beautiful ivory carving in a shop window. He couldn't get it out of his mind, and each day as he passed the shop, the urge to return to carving grew more compelling. It was something he simply had to do. He left the restaurant, and a whole new life began for him. He had to resume his studies, and once again he was very poor. His marriage broke up, but his creative urge was so great that he continued to study, doing rough carving (*arabori*) to support himself and his two sons. His interest began to center on netsuke, and every spare moment was spent in working toward his goal of becoming a top-ranking netsuke carver. Finally, in 1965 he took the first netsuke bearing his signature Shodo into the Sunamoto shop. They were excellent. In fact, Mr. Sunamoto says that Shodo has never brought in a netsuke that wasn't top quality.

Like Hokusai, Shodo keeps a beautiful sketchbook. Here his netsuke designs are worked out in detail before he starts to bring them to life in ivory. Unlike Ryushi, who usually carves feminine figures, Shodo invariably includes a man's figure in his designs. His subjects are drawn from customs and folktales of old Japan: Hana-Saka Jijii, a nobleman in a palanquin, two gods playing *go* (Figs. 38, 86, 99). He is constantly challenged by trying to do the impossible with his carver's tools. And that is what he does—the impossible. He is a master of meticulous detail, but his artistry comes through above the force of the techniques and mechanics. Technique never becomes an end in itself. He conveys much in a small space, but his netsuke are quiet and his faces have serene beauty.

Life is now much brighter for Shodo. He is established as a first-rank netsuke carver, and he has remarried and moved to a suburb of Tokyo, away from much of the noise and confusion of the city. He likes people and makes friends easily, often bringing them home—people from all walks of life: a policeman or a merchant, an artisan or a person of prominence. He sometimes delights his wife by cooking delicious European dishes, never Japanese food. His ability to work with his hands often finds expression in making furniture for his home. His older son has gone into the business world. In fact, already he is making more money than Shodo. The younger son has not yet made his choice of a career. At the moment, his greatest interest is playing the guitar.

Shodo's love of old Japan extends beyond netsuke subjects. He has a great interest in antiques and knows many antique dealers whom he visits on the day he takes his finished work to the Sunamoto shop.

His hobby is the growing of *bonsai*. He finds it very relaxing as well as restful for his eyes. He also finds in it the Japanese sense of harmony between nature and art. And Shodo is a master of his art—the art of netsuke carving.

Rakumin—Seimin—Shomin—Shodo

151. Shodo at work.

SHOGETSU

The thousands of tourists who have bought a netsuke with a movable face as a memento of Japan will be especially interested in Shogetsu. He is the carver who originated the revolving-head technique, now often copied by less skilled carvers. The sophisticated collector may have little interest in "trick" netsuke per se, but he quickly recognizes a Shogetsu for its technical perfection, its rather elaborate composition with skillfully etched decorative patterns, and its beautifully polished and softly stained finish. *Sumi* ink is used to accent the hairdress and elaborate garment patterns of his netsuke, and he uses no primary colors. His subjects are taken from the life and customs of his people: a folk dancer (Fig. 40), a mother and child, a man tending *bonsai* (Fig. 84), a puppeteer. His style, his workmanship, and his designs are easily identified. Shogetsu was one of the first contemporary carvers to be recognized among foreign collectors.

Shogetsu, born Kikuo Amano, started to learn to carve at the turn of the century, when he was only thirteen. He first studied under Miyazaki, working with the bones of cows. As Westerners began to show interest in netsuke and *okimono*, and exports started passing through Yokohama harbor, more students turned to ivory carving. Among them was young Kikuo, who apprenticed himself to Shungetsu, an expert in ivory figure carving, from whom he later received the professional name Shogetsu.

Shungetsu was a rigid disciplinarian and difficult taskmaster. When his pupils were assigned complicated projects requiring long hours and great patience, they would often nod with fatigue. The master would then force them to pierce their thighs with a gimletlike tool in order to stay awake and continue their work.

Currently in his late eighties and despite high blood pressure and some of the infirmities of old age, Shogetsu is still producing beautiful netsuke. He is deeply concerned with the preservation of the art of netsuke carving and feels that the best chance of keeping the art alive lies in the carver's own blood line, since the apprenticeship system and carving "schools" are almost institutions of the past. Two of his five sons (there are also two daughters) learned to carve. One of them was killed during the war. The other carver-son, Yasuo, is known by his artist name, Shofu. He and his family live with Shogetsu, and he is as dedicated as his father to preserving the art of netsuke carving. For this reason

152. Shogetsu (*foreground*) in studio with his son Shofu.

he spends time teaching carving skills to Shogetsu's grandsons. Shofu is a fine carver himself, relying largely on finish carving (*shiage*) to support his family. If he could devote more time to netsuke designing and carving, he could become a great carver like his father. Shofu is a very honest, extremely hard-working person and is active in J.I.S.A. But he still finds time to produce beautiful calligraphy.

Shogetsu is almost a recluse. His whole life revolves around designing and carving netsuke and occasionally *okimono*. When dealers come to the house, Shofu talks to them. Shigeo Tsujita, his agent, was the only person who could easily see Shogetsu, and he arranged for us to see him in the fall of 1969. We have since learned that we were the first collectors Shogetsu had ever met.

We were greeted at the door by Shofu and ushered into a rather large room. In the middle of the room, Shogetsu sat on a cushion on the tatami floor in front of a low tea table. In quite correct Japanese etiquette, he remained seated, bowing low to greet us. At the same table, Shofu's wife graciously served Japanese green tea and refreshments.

Shogetsu is an unusually tall, broad-shouldered man for a Japanese of his age, and he looked very regal in his erect, cross-legged posture. In front of him were many items of interest to a netsuke collector: old, well-worn copies of original Hokusai sketchbooks; small and simple basic netsuke designs in wood, carved by his teacher; and nearby, a hand drill and scores upon scores of handmade carving tools. He particularly called our attention to the very fine-pointed tool he pushes with his thumb in doing his pattern etching and to the difference in the tools used when working with and against the grain of the ivory. Occasional ideas may come from a sketchbook, but Shogetsu's designs are his own and are clearly drawn in his mind. He never sketches a netsuke design on paper before starting to carve, nor does he make clay models.

It was a memorable afternoon. Usually, Shogetsu gives of himself only through his artistry and skill. After leaving him that day, we felt we had not only met one of the first-rank netsuke carvers of the twentieth century but had also had a glimpse of the fine, dedicated person behind the dignified, reserved artist.

Shungetsu—Shogetsu—Shofu

153. Shoko.

昇
己 SHOKO

In the spring of 1971, my friend Michi telephoned Shoko to tell him about the book on contemporary carvers I was writing and to see if we could come to visit him. He explained that he had been ill for several years but was sure he would recover and carve again. He talked to Michi for fully thirty minutes. He was most enthusiastic about the idea of my book and was hopeful of being able to see me when I returned to Tokyo in the fall. When Michi called late in October, his wife sadly told her that Shoko had passed away on October 15.

As a very young man, Shotaro Nishino wanted to become a painter and showed particular interest and talent in watercolors. Fortunately for the world of netsuke, his aunt, who was married to Soko Morita, persuaded him to become a carver. At fifteen, he started to study under Soko and, as Shoko, became one of the great carvers of the So school. He was the most original of Soko's pupils, and from his fertile and eccentric imagination came many designs that probably only he fully understood. He believed that an artist must be infused with a pure and holy spirit before he starts to create, and he worshipped each day at a Buddhist temple. His wife and his sister-in-law firmly believe he was possessed of "god-spirit."

Shoko would spend days, sometimes weeks, studying all aspects of his subject—the metaphysical connotations, the religious and historical meanings. He then would make a detailed sketch and a clay model. With consummate skill and painstaking labor, he would seldom spend less, and usually more, than three months on a single netsuke. He carved only at night, seven nights a week. Knowing how little carvers were paid during most of his professional life, I asked his wife how they lived on what he earned. She gave me a resigned little smile and said she had opened a small tea store where she made enough to take care of their basic needs. She said that Shoko was not interested in money —his whole life was carving. Beyond that, he ate, slept, and read the paper.

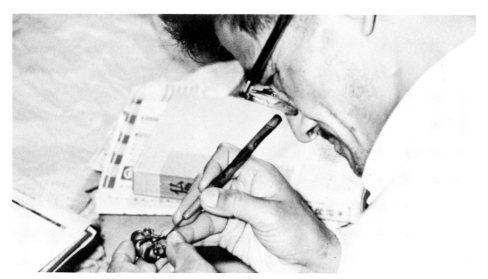

154. Shoko at work.

She couldn't even get him to take a walk. She said that most carvers today cannot spend so much time on their netsuke, since they want a better life for themselves and their families.

Shoko worked almost exclusively in wood and never repeated a design. If a dealer brought him a picture of a subject and commissioned him to copy it, he would do his own conception of the subject. He refused to make exact copies. Ghosts and *bakemono* were favorite subjects of his and showed Shoko's innate sense of fun. He often did *rakan* or some of the Seven Gods of Good Fortune, as well as Buddhas, but always with great originality. Occasionally he did designs from nature. One of the most beautiful netsuke I have ever seen is a group of small gourds carved from fawn-colored wood, which was his wedding gift to his wife.

During the last years of his life, until he became ill, Shoko devoted most of his energies to carving small Buddhist statues. The most famous of these figures is an eight-inch Senju (Thousand-armed) Kannon carved from a single piece of sandalwood. Shoko spent between three and four years on this piece, and each of the forty-two arms was carefully studied through every source available. He then employed the netsuke technique in carving the tiny figures held in each hand. Avery Brundage heard of this piece of sculpture and wanted to buy it, according to Mrs. Nishino, but it had been commissioned by an art collector in the Yokohama area as a gift for his wife.

It is sad that the life of an artist of such skill and talent should have been cut short at fifty-six. Shoko will always be considered one of the great netsuke carvers of the twentieth century.

Hojitsu—Kojitsu—Joso—Soko (Morita)—Shoko

SOSUI

A Sosui netsuke is always one of the proudest possessions of a collector whether a sophisticated purist, an amateur, or a collector of contemporary netsuke. "Which is your favorite netsuke?" I recently asked a friend who owns more than two thousand netsuke, a collection composed largely of antique netsuke. He said he had two favorites: one an antique piece and the other a Sosui. Another collector decided that he would liquidate his collection rather than leave it to his estate. This he did, keeping only thirty for his own enjoyment. All thirty were Sosuis.

The carvers of the so-called So school were important among the group of carver-teachers who helped to preserve the art of netsuke carving in its finest tradition after the netsuke was no longer a part of Japanese attire and before the worldwide collectors' demand for netsuke had developed. Joso, the first of this group of So artists, was born in Tokyo in 1855. Joso has very special sentimental significance in my life, because the first gift I ever received from my husband was a small exquisite *okimono* of Urashima, carved by Joso. While stationed in Tokyo immediately after the end of World War II, he had found it in a shop in the Imperial Hotel arcade. He then knew nothing about ivory carving, *okimono,* or netsuke. He only knew this was a carving that to a high degree embodied his criteria for good art: brevity, beauty, simplicity, and restraint. It wasn't until we had become addicted to netsuke collecting, many years later, that we learned it had been carved by Joso.

Two of Joso's best pupils were Gyokuso and Soko Morita, both born in 1879. They were warm friends and from 1920 to 1934 met daily to study netsuke together. When Gyokuso's oldest son, Jiro Ouchi, born in 1911, showed artistic talent, Gyokuso asked his friend Soko to take him as a pupil. For ten years, Jiro (soon to be known to the netsuke world as Sosui) studied under Soko and became a great artist in his own right.

Sosui, who died in 1972, was one of the very few first-rank carvers of the twentieth century preferring wood as their medium. He often combined different kinds of wood, or wood and ivory. These, together with pieces containing bits of mother-of-pearl or other inlay, he called his "mosaic netsuke" (Figs. 4, 33). Occasionally, he made a netsuke in ivory, no less skillfully executed but usually simpler, less detailed, than his wood netsuke. Some of his ivory and ebony netsuke are stylized, almost abstract (Figs. 10, 20). It was not unusual for Sosui to spend a month or six weeks on some of his earlier pieces.

155. Sosui.

Many of his more complex netsuke are quite delicate and open in composition, deviating from the basic guidelines of the functional antique netsuke and yet remaining completely acceptable to netsuke purists. In some repects he was guided by tradition, but he never allowed its influence to obscure his originality or his lively imagination, which occasionally showed a modern sense of design. His highly detailed pieces are a showcase for his incomparable mechanical and technical skill with the carver's knives, but their fundamental simplicity and beauty of design remain dominant. His subjects were usually taken from Japanese life and customs, animals and nature, rather than from folktales.

I first met Sosui in the spring of 1970, after learning that he was ill and had been unable to carve for several years. After my friend and interpreter Michi Matsumoto had explained that I was writing a book on living netsuke carvers, Sosui's wife assured her that he would be pleased to see us later that week. She gave Michi and me a warm welcome at the gate of their modest home, saying that the anticipation of our visit had put new life into her husband. As we entered the typical Japanese living room, we saw Sosui sitting on his *futon* (mattress) at the far side of the room. He looked toward us eagerly, his dark eyes so intense we were scarcely aware of his other features. In spite of years of illness, he looked younger than his age. He was bedridden and spoke with difficulty but was very alert and most enthusiastic over the prospect of a book being written on contemporary netsuke carvers.

Although he was no longer able to carve, his face lighted up whenever the word "netsuke" was mentioned. A small TV set, placed high so he could see it while lying down, helped to fill the long hours when his wife was away at work. His only companion during most of the day was a green-eyed Maltese cat. In spite of their problems, Mrs. Ouchi showed herself to be a warm, uncomplaining woman devoted to her husband and their two grown daughters.

I asked Sosui which of all of his designs was his favorite. He replied, "Cuttlefish in a Basket." This delighted me, for it is the subject of my favorite among our Sosui netsuke (Fig. 4).

The ownership of a Sosui netsuke goes beyond the pride of knowing that it was created by one of the greatest netsuke carvers of all time. It gives the collector a warmth of personal pleasure that completes the trinity of creative spirit that passes from the artist to his work and, in turn, to the owner.

Hojitsu—Kojitsu—Joso—Soko (Morita)—Sosui

YOKO

In our own world of netsuke collecting, Yoko will always have a special place, for it was he who carved the first netsuke my husband and I ever bought (Fig. 51). It was years later that we learned it was a contemporary netsuke and that Yoko (or Kyokusen, as our netsuke was signed) had carved it. We knew nothing about netsuke at the time. We simply bought it as a typically Japanese piece of miniature sculpture, beautiful in design and superb in workmanship. A decade and a half and three hundred netsuke later, it is still one of our favorite netsuke and one of our best.

Yoko's death in 1974 was a great loss for us. Born in 1885, he started to carve when he was twelve, working and learning under his father, Ryusai, one of several outstanding carvers who had studied under the master Shungetsu. The Komada family is famous in the world of ivory carving. Besides his father, Yoko's brother, Ryusui was a carver and teacher, and Ryusui's two sons, Ryushi and Ryuho, are the youngest members of the Komada family to carry on the family tradition—Ryushi for his netsuke and Ryuho for his *okimono*.

156. Yoko.

Yoko had no children but took much pride in his two nephews and had great influence on them and their art.

For many years, Shigeo Tsujita acted as agent for much of Yoko's work, and all of his carvings that were sold through Tsujita were signed Kyokusen. Tsujita was more than an agent to the carvers whose work he handled. He was also their close personal friend. Every spring, for many years, Tsujita took his wife, Hakusei and his wife, Ichiro and his adopted daughter, and Yoko and his wife's sister (after his wife's death) to some place in Japan on a holiday, paying all the bills himself. Needless to say, Tsujita's guests looked forward with great anticipation each year to this gay outing.

Yoko's own serene, happy disposition is reflected in both his netsuke and his *okimono*. He often used a touch of color on the ivory, and his netsuke are always tranquil and pleasing as well as expertly carved. They are usually figures in repose rather than in motion and are derived from Japanese or Chinese folktales or genre subjects. Always they have originality and beauty.

His warm sense of humor is illustrated by his choice of the story of Taikobo as an *okimono* subject. Taikobo, the Chinese astrologer, geographer, and military expert of the twelfth century B.C., is often depicted fishing but without float, hook, or bait. He wanted to escape from his nagging wife in order to ponder his problems surrounded by nature's calm.

Yoko was a short, wiry man with merry, twinkling eyes, and a happy grin. His warmth of heart was felt by those meeting him for the first time as well as by old friends. Even in old age he carved more than six hours a day and spent his holidays thinking about new designs. I asked him when he was going to retire. He replied without hesitation: "I can never stop carving. The secret of long life is to be poor and to work every day, because that will keep you healthy."

Shungetsu—Ryusai—Yoko

YOSHIYUKI

Yoshiyuki Shibata died as he had lived, carving a netsuke. On December 28, 1970, at the age of seventy-seven, he sat on the tatami mat carving a netsuke. From the next room, with a *shoji* partition between them, his wife, Hatsuko, could see his shadow as he worked. Suddenly, the figure silhouetted against the screen slumped forward. Hatsuko rushed to him, but he was gone, the little unfinished netsuke still grasped in his hand.

Yoshiyuki was a very shy, gentle, withdrawn man. Although he had friends among his contemporaries in the carving world—Ichiro, Gaho, Hakuraku, and Yoko—he neither sought nor encouraged social contacts. He worked seven days a week and usually spent fifteen days on a single netsuke. Carving was literally his life. Fishing was his only relaxation. But even when he was sitting on the riverbank with pole in hand, his mind constantly sought new design ideas.

Always true to the old tradition of netsuke carving, his netsuke have great tactile appeal or "good feeling," as the Japanese say; are interestingly and amusingly designed from old legends or real-life animals; and were executed with meticulous attention to detail. They have a softness that was not explained until after his death. For centuries there had been great secretiveness among netsuke carvers over individual techniques, and one of the best-kept secrets was the way Yoshiyuki achieved the color of stain without staining and a softness absent in most stained ivory. He placed his ivory netsuke above burning incense until it had taken on the desired shade. The lingering scent of incense could be detected on a Yoshiyuki netsuke for some time after it was finished.

Most Yoshiyuki netsuke were sold in the Hakusui ivory shops in Tokyo and Yokohama. The president of this company, Y. Watanabe, says that a number of years ago, when these netsuke had become popular with collectors, he told Yoshiyuki he should receive more money for his work. Yoshiyuki's selfless reply was short and certainly not attuned to Japan's inflated standard of living today: "I get along very well. I have everything I need or want. Why should you pay me more?"

The netsuke world lost one of the great artists of the twentieth century when the heart and the carving fingers of Yoshiyuki were stilled.

Tomochika—Nobuchika—Nobuyuki—Nobuyoshi—Yoshiyuki

YUKIMASA

One of the rare husband-and-wife teams in the netsuke carving world, Yukimasa (Tadami Uno) and his wife, Harue, live in a comfortable home in Nagara, Gifu City.

Like most young boys of his generation with artistic leanings, Yukimasa wanted to be a great painter and at the age of twelve left regular school to study art. Several years later he met the fine Kyoto netsuke carver Koshin Akiyama, and, after seeing a number of his netsuke, Yukimasa knew netsuke carving had to be his vocation too. Koshin took him as a pupil in May 1929, and they worked together for eleven years. Yukimasa learned both wood and ivory carving and particularly likes to carve animals and man figures of the Edo period. It is interesting to note that when he carves animals, he uses the name of the famous Gifu animal carver Tomoichi. His "middle" works he signs Masatomo, but his best netsuke are always signed Yukimasa.

It had been his dream that his son would become a great carver, but the long learning period posed a real economic problem, what with today's living costs. Instead, Shintaro became an English teacher in senior high school. Yukimasa's wife wanted to learn to become a carver in order to share that very large segment of her husband's life. She was not skillful in carving but did become very proficient in the staining, polishing, and coloring stages of netsuke making. Today, she does all of this work for her husband, saving him countless hours that he can use in designing and carving. His Hokusai-like sketchbook contains hundreds of detailed drawings of Yukimasa netsuke—past, present, and future.

His studio reflects the many-faceted nature of Yukimasa's interests. One side of the room is lined with rather extensive stereo equipment, another wall has floor-to-ceiling bookshelves containing many English volumes (his son's) and much poetry (Yukimasa is a *tanka* poet). On top of the record-playing equipment, arranged in good taste, are a number of excellent pieces of Japanese ceramics. A delicate flower arrangement shows his wife's contribution to a beautiful, serene room.

Yukimasa generally carves in ivory but occasionally makes a wood netsuke, using boxwood. All of his output is marketed through Mr. Yokoyama, of Kyoto. He is not very well known in Japan, since eighty to ninety percent of his netsuke

157. Yukimasa and his wife.

are exported for foreign markets. His designs are good, usually original versions of old familiar subjects. His animals and birds are extremely well done, and all of his carving is meticulous, with great integrity of detail.

When Yukimasa was in his early teens, he developed a serious stammering affliction. He was determined not to go through life with this handicap and enrolled in a school for correction of stammering. His training there was long and difficult, but he finally recovered his uninhibited speech. When he has difficult carving days and remembers the easier art of painting, he recalls the rough period he went through in conquering his speech impediment and says to himself, "Nothing is impossible if your will is strong enough."

友光 YUKO

If only two words were used to describe Toshitake Nakamura, they would be "energy" and "enthusiasm." Yuko (his artist name) has been secretary of the J.I.S.A. for several years, and nothing is too much work for him if he feels it is for the good of the association and beneficial to the future of the art and profession of ivory carving. Although the J.I.S.A. is a young organization, its strength today can be credited to the vision of its founders and the ability and unselfish effort contributed by officers like Yuko.

He is equally enthusiastic and dedicated in his netsuke carving. He also carves

158. Yuko.

okimono, on which he uses the *go* Somei, but since the war he has devoted most of his time to netsuke. He generally works with ivory but occasionally makes a netsuke in wood (boxwood, sandalwood, or cherry) or in wood with ivory touches (Fig. 37) or wood with mother-of-pearl inlay. His subjects cover a wide range, including figures of Edo-period men, figures from contemporary life, and all kinds of nature subjects. His animals and insects are particularly popular with collectors. He carves with skill and adheres basically to the traditional netsuke in form and composition.

Yuko works ten hours a day, six days a week, unless he is involved in some J.I.S.A. project or is helping a fellow carver. He finds relaxation on his day off in gardening, swimming, baseball, or movies. He is an outgoing person with a quick sense of humor.

Some netsuke artists are consumed with their own creativeness—their painstaking, time-consuming workmanship in producing masterpieces to the exclusion of outside activities and social contacts. Others, like Yuko, are deeply concerned with the practical aspects of keeping netsuke art alive, and they give generously of their time to this problem. The world of netsuke needs both.

Shungetsu—Harushige—Bishu (Saito)—Teruichiro (Saito)—Shosai (Saito)—Yuko

Appendices

List of Contemporary Netsuke Carvers

BAFUNZAN UMAROKU

BISHU
(MISHU)

KEY TO ABBREVIATIONS

A.N.: actual name   W.: wife's name
F.:   father's name   C.: names of children
G.: grandfather's name

BAFUNZAN UMAROKU 馬糞山馬六. A.N.: Kodo Okuda. Born September 15, 1940, in Tokyo. F.: Kodo Okuda (ivory carver). G: Genjiro Okuda (ivory dealer). W.: Yukie. C.: Chikatoshi, Genjiro. Uses signatures Kodo 浩堂 and Shojin 正人 on *okimono* and other ivory sculptures. Learned ivory carving from his father and became particularly interested in the world of humor in the Edo period. Had been trained as a painter before turning to carving. In larger pieces specializes in plants, flowers, and birds. His netsuke are all original designs taken from contemporary Japanese life and are sometimes erotic. Usually works from ten to fifteen hours a day, seven days a week. Hobbies: traveling, reading, and going to museums on rare days off. Member of several art and painting associations.

BISHU 美洲. A.N.: Katsutoshi Saito. Born April 28, 1943, in Tokyo. F.: Shosai Saito (ivory carver and teacher). G.: Teruichiro Saito. Started to learn to carve from his father when he was seventeen. Skillful carver, very imaginative and innovative, most of his netsuke bordering on the abstract. Definitely one of the best of young carvers. During the first quarter of this century, his grandfather founded a production group whose work was signed Baisho or Baishodo. The group was carried on by Bishu's father, who once employed more than forty carvers. Bishu has phased out this group and is carving only *issaku* netsuke. Member of J.I.S.A. and Chowa-kai.

214

CHIKUSAI   GAHO   GASHO   GENDO   GODO

CHIKUSAI 竹斉. A.N.: Kyojiro Saito. Born July 30, 1899, in Kawagoe, Saitama Prefecture. Father was an architect. G.: Taketaro Saito. W.: Chiyo. C.: Hiroshi, Masashi, Toshiharu, Masahiko, Setsuko. Has been carving since age of eighteen; studied under Matsutaro Shimomura. Carves only in ivory. Subjects taken from nature and from Japanese life and customs. Was a radio repairman during World War II and is a ham radio operator. Hobby: growing bonsai. Member of J.I.S.A.

GAHO 雅邦. A.N.: Shunji Imai. Born in Tokyo, 1901. F.: Hei Imai. W.: Fujiko. C.: Kuniyoshi, Kyoji, Mineko, Terumi, Reiko, Toshiaki. Studied under Jitsuga, originator of the ivory clamshell with detailed inside carvings, and became fourth master of the Hakumin (Sekine) school, founded by Hakumin, who came from a samurai clan. Has been carving since he was fifteen years old, except for a period during World War II when he worked in a military factory. Has a pupil, Gamei, who shows promise as a carver. Likes to design from ukiyoe subjects; best known for his *tanemaki* (sower), Urashima, and *soryo* (Buddhist priest) netsuke. Yoshiyuki, Ichiro, and Gaho are close friends and sometimes collaborate in making groups of figures like the Seven Gods of Good Fortune. Uses considerable color. Prewar netsuke smaller and more delicate than later ones; all well carved, with honest attention to details of clothing and mores, facial expressions, and traditional netsuke forms. Member of J.I.S.A.

GASHO 雅生. A.N.: Masakazu Kobari. Born August 28, 1944, in Tokyo. Studied under Toshikatsu Kobari. Subject: figures of men. Member of J.I.S.A.

GENDO 弦道. A.N.: Yoneo Tamura. Born September 15, 1935, in Ibaraki Prefecture. W.: Hiroko. C.: Kyoko. Studied under Hosei. Does rough carving but spends as much time as possible creating netsuke designs based on manners of the Edo period and the Meiji era. Hobbies: growing bonsai and taking care of birds. Member of J.I.S.A.

GODO 悟堂. A.N.: Goichiro Abe. Born September 30, 1914, in Tochigi Prefecture. F.: Yonezo Abe. G.: Tokuzo Abe. W.: Fuji. C.: Takashi, Kenji, Mariko. Studied under Takahashi Katsuzo.

GYOKUDO　GYOKUGETSU　GYOKUSHO　GYOKUYUKI　HAKURAKU

GYOKUDO 玉堂. A.N.: Shozo Suzuki. Born January 20, 1910, in Tokyo. F.: Kametaro Suzuki. G.: Iwakichi Suzuki. W.: Ryoko. C.: Ritsuko (ivory carver), Mitsuko, Masaaki. Studied under Gyokukan Suzuki. Member of J.I.S.A.

GYOKUGETSU 玉月 (SEIGETSU 清月). A.N.: Kaneharu Yamada. Born May 15, 1902, in Nagoya. F.: Sozaemon Yamada. W.: Hana. C.: Akira, Katsuyo, Tamotsu. Studied under his father, Gyokudo Suzuki. Carves only ivory. Best-known subjects: *sennin* and Seven Gods of Good Fortune. Member of J.I.S.A., Aisen-kai, and Chowa-kai.

GYOKUSHO 玉昇. A.N.: Toshio Suzuki. Born January 23, 1940, in Tokyo. F.: Kametaro Suzuki. G.: Iwakichi Suzuki. W.: Yoshie. C.: Kazuo, Akio. Studied under Gyokukan. Recently devoting more time to netsuke and someday may be a fine carver. Member of J.I.S.A.

GYOKUYUKI. 玉之. A.N.: Tomio Suzuki. Born November 2, 1924, in Tokyo. Father was a farmer. G.: Kametaro Suzuki. W.: Kazue. C.: Minoru, Tamiko. Carves flowers on *manju* and figures of old men from ukiyoe. Has been carving netsuke since 1965 and shows considerable progress. Member of J.I.S.A.

HAKURAKU 白楽. A.N.: Harutaro Matsuda. Born March 11, 1890, in Kyobashi, Tokyo; lived in Yokohama; died February 19, 1974. G.: Naotaro Matsuda. W.: Shizu. C.: Michiteru, Hiroshi. Studied under Doraku (Yoshida) and began to specialize in netsuke in the early 1950s. Used very little color, sometimes none at all. Designs are simple and strong. Subject matter usually women and children but is most famous for his sumo wrestlers. Contemporary and friend of Ichiro and Gaho and sometimes collaborated with them in making groups of figures like the Seven Gods of Good Fortune. Father and teacher of Michiteru, also an ivory carver. Member of J.I.S.A.

HAKUSEI 白生. A.N.: Teikichi Nagai. Born September 15, 1905, in Chiba Prefecture. F.: Yasunosuke Nagai. G.: Kidayu Nagai. W.: Toshiko. C.: Reiko, Masakazu (the carver Kosen), Teiji. Oldest sister was married to Ryusui Komada, whose sons

HAKUSEI   HAKUZAN   HIDEMITSU   HIDEYUKI (KOSEI)   HODO

are both carvers: Ryushi and Ryuho. Studied carving under Ryusui Komada and Yoko Komada. Occasionally carves netsuke but specializes in carving *okimono*. Worked in an aircraft factory during World War II. Member of J.I.S.A. (president, 1971–72) and Aisen-kai.

HAKUZAN 伯山. A.N.: Takashi Sugeno. Born September 17, 1935, in Fukushima Prefecture. Descended from a samurai family. G.: Ukichi Honda. W.: Kimiko. C.: Yasuyo, Keiko. Studied under Aisaburo Hara and Meido Inoue. Material: ivory. Subjects from ukiyoe. Not yet an *issaku* carver. Member of J.I.S.A.

HIDEMITSU 秀光. A.N.: Seiichi Ito. Born September 7, 1914, in Chiba Prefecture. Studied under Sosai Yoshida. Favorite subject: Okubo Hikozaemon.

HIDEYUKI (KOSEI) 英之 (廣晴). A.N.: Hideo Sakurai. Born October 6, 1941, in Tokyo. F.: Hirokichi Sakurai (Kosei). G.: Chomatsu Sakurai. W.: Masako. One of the top-ranking young carvers showing promise. Usually carves in ivory with a minimum of color; also does excellent work in wood with lacquer and inlay decoration. Delicate and detailed technique. Subjects are usually Japanese legendary figures. Member of J.I.S.A. and Chowa-kai.

HODO 芳堂. A.N.: Yoshio Sekizawa. Born July 27, 1929, in Yokosuka, Kanagawa Prefecture. F.: Ko Sekizawa. G.: Shozo Sekizawa. W.: Taeko. C.: Hiroaki. Graduated from Kanagawa Prefectural Training School of Commerce and Industry. After working for the Toyo Electric Company for two years, became interested in ivory carving and resigned his position. Began to study fundamentals of the art of ivory carving and in 1950 entered the private school of the great artist-carver Hodo Nakamura. He soon mastered the carving of figurines and figures of Kannon, the specialty of the school. This training is seen in the Buddhist, Kabuki, and Noh figures he draws upon for his *okimono* subjects. He was directly endowed with his master's signature Hodo in attestation of his authenticity and his worthiness to be the school's next master. In netsuke carving, his subjects are usually drawn from the everyday world: an old man, a fisherman, a sandalmaker, a carpenter, a man with masks selling tea cakes. His netsuke are simple but display careful attention to detail,

HOSEI

HOSHU (KEISEKI)

HOZAN (YOSHIDA)

HOZAN (FUJITA)

sometimes gentle, sometimes delicate, but always strong. He often uses dark colors for contrast in the attire of his figures. Anatomically, these figures are superb; artistically, they are serenely beautiful. Has participated in an exhibition of ivory carvings by four contemporary artists, an exhibition known as the Zokeiten, and various exhibitions sponsored by the Sunamoto Ivory Shop. His designs are taken from genre or traditional subject matter but are always individual and original. May repeat a subject, but always with variations in design. Also known for his outstanding *okimono*. Hobbies: swimming, playing *go,* fishing, and traveling.

HOSEI 芳清. A.N.: Seiichi Ishii. Born January 1, 1926, in Gumma Prefecture. F.: Kumesaku Ishii. Studied under Hosei Meguro. Material: ivory. Carves mostly *okimono*. Member of J.I.S.A.

HOSHU 芳朱. A.N.: Tsuyoshi Yamagata. Born September 10, 1932, in Tokyo. G.: Tokuzo Yamagata. W.: Tamiko. C.: Naoko, Takeshi. Has been carving since 1948. Learned from Hakusei, who lived in his neighborhood. Feels it is important to preserve old things, and his designs are based on Japanese life and customs. Material: ivory. Uses signature Keiseki 桂石 on *okimono*. Hobbies: collecting and caring for cactuses, cycling from spring to autumn, listening to popular and classical music. Member of J.I.S.A.

HOZAN 芳山. A.N.: Kunio Yoshida. Born September 7, 1921, in Tokyo. Descendant of the shogun Takauji Ashikaga. F.: Akizumi Yoshida. W.: Sadako. C.: Mitsuharu, Yukari. Likes to carve genre subjects: old man, parent and child. Formerly often carved trick netsuke. Considerably more than an average carver; shows promise of one day reaching top rank. Hobby: caring for goldfish and plants. Member of J.I.S.A.

HOZAN 寶山. A.N.: Shigeo Fujita. Born March 15, 1917, in Taito-ku, Tokyo; now living in Chiba Prefecture. F.: Kando Fujita. G.: Kansai Asai. W.: Setsuko. C.: Yaeko, Yuji. Carving lineage from famous master Hojitsu. Also poet and calligrapher. Original netsuke designs, but dominated by traditional form and subject matter. Detailed and skilled workmanship. Best-known subjects: Hotei, male figures from old Japanese legends, and contemporary genre occupations. Received an award

ICHIO   ICHIRO   IPPO   KANGYOKU
                                            (RISSHISAI)

from prewar Ministry of Commerce and Industry. Considered a first-rank twentieth-century carver. Hobbies: walking and bowling. Member of J.I.S.A. and Aisen-kai.

ICHIO 一桜. A.N.: Niro Sakurai. Born April 15, 1923, in Tokyo. Descended from a samurai family. F.: Seiun Sakurai. G.: Chomatsu Sakurai. W.: Yoko. C.: Shitomi, Kiyotaka. His uncle Kosei and his cousin Hideyuki are both carvers. Learned to carve from his father. Sometimes carves figures in stylized fashion; other Ichio netsuke depict complicated Japanese folktales. Known for his subject "Garden of Love." Very versatile artist and carves with great technical precision. Also a Japanese-style painter. Active member of J.I.S.A. and one of its founders.

ICHIRO 一郎. A.N.: Ichiro Inada. Born March 17, 1891, in Tokyo. F.: Fukutaro Inada. C.: Nobuko. Studied under Koichi, whose carving lineage goes back to Hojitsu. Started to learn to carve at thirteen, but always interested in painting. First carver to use color extensively on ivory. Early in his career, often carved animal subjects but is best known for his figures from Kabuki plays, Japanese history, and everyday life. Particularly enjoys carving figures of children. Usually carves in ivory, but the wooden netsuke he carved during World War II are often considered his finest works. Designs original, strong, and somewhat stylized, with considerable use of color; skillful workmanship without being excessively intricate. Warm, outgoing personality and generous with his time in helping young carvers. Very active in J.I.S.A. and often considered dean of older living carvers. He says his hobby is carving netsuke.

IPPO 一峰. A.N.: Chusaburo Furusawa. Born January 31, 1910, in Tochigi Prefecture. F.: Kameiemon Furusawa, G.: Ushinosuke Furusawa. W.: Kiku. C.: Tadao, Takeyoshi, Tomoto, Shizue, Mitsue.

KANGYOKU 寛玉. A.N.: Noriyoshi Tachihara. Born January 6, 1944, in Tokyo. F.: Fusakichi (Kangyoku) Tachihara (died 1963), who carved *okimono* but very few netsuke. G.: Ichitaro Tachihara. W.: Naomi. C.: Tomomi. Learned carving from his father, who belonged to the school originated by the distinguished artist of the Meiji era Hojitsu Yamada. Adheres to traditional antique-netsuke guidelines in form

KANKO   KANSHO   KARHU   KAZUHIDE

and techniques but very innovative in design, many of his netsuke bordering on the surrealist or abstract. His specialty is animals: *shishi*, puppies, rats, squirrels, horses, rabbits, monkeys. His unstained, beautifully polished white rabbit, with coral eyes, is a great favorite, and one example of this design was purchased by the Empress of Japan in 1967. His designs are bold, sometimes whimsical or amusing, and exceptional in tactile quality. In 1973, began to use the *go* Risshisai Kangyoku 立志斎寛玉 on some of his netsuke. *Risshisai* is a Buddhist word with various connotations: "determination to be the best," "going from lowest to highest," and "rising in the world." One of the most popular of the young twentieth-century carvers. Hobbies: golf and other sports, reading, and hiking. Member of J.I.S.A.

KANKO 寛弘. A.N.: Keizo Ebina. Born March 7, 1921, in Hirosaki, Aomori Prefecture. F.: Katsutaro Ebina. G.: Mitsujiro Ebina. W.: Teruko. C.: Masaru. Served in army from 1942 to 1947. Started to carve in 1955. Studied under Hiro-o Asai. Designs are original and usually based on animal subjects; most popular: *shishi* and cow. Material: ivory. Hobby: walking. Member of J.I.S.A. and Aisen-kai.

KANSHO 寛章. A.N.: Hiroshi Satake. Born July 9, 1915, in Tokyo. F.: Kozaburo Satake. Grandfather was a samurai. W.: Sadami. C.: Yasuko, Akie. Studied under Kanji Asai. Material: ivory. Original designs, mostly of animals. Worked in an office during World War II. Member of J.I.S.A.

KARHU 佳風. Full name: Clifton Karhu. Born in 1927 in Duluth, Minnesota. W.: Lois. Three children. Served in Japan during the occupation; later studied at Minneapolis School of Art. Returned to Japan to live in 1955 and now resides permanently in Kyoto. One of Japan's leading woodblock-print artists. Avocation: netsuke carving (Fig. 21).

KAZUHIDE 一英. A.N.: Eiichi Murata. Born March 31, 1924, in Tokyo. F.: Kokichi Murata. W.: Matsue. C.: Yoko, Osamu. Material: ivory. Studied under his father, who was a fine carver. Subject: figures of men. Member of J.I.S.A.

KEIUN 桂雲. A.N.: Minosuke Omura. Born June 25, 1912, in Fushimi-ku, Kyoto;

KEIUN   KENJI   KODO   KOETSU

now living in Uji. F.: Minosuke Omura. G.: Nihei Omura. W.: Tomiko. C.: Asako. As a very young man, Keiun studied under Mitsutami Tsuji, who was not a netsuke carver, and learned to carve *okimono*, especially *to-bijin* (statues of beauties of T'ang-dynasty China). To Keiun, this seemed no longer to be real art. He left his teacher and made the rounds of museums and exhibitions in an effort to find an art form more meaningful to him—one that expressed more of the true artistry of Japan. He soon decided that the netsuke was the best form for ivory carving. At that time he was eighteen years old, and he then began his outstanding career as a netsuke carver, studying and working by himself. He was particularly influenced by Kaigyokusai, as is evident in his animal netsuke. He is best known for his "Cleaning the Buddha" subject, which depicts the annual cleaning of the 53.5-foot Nara Daibutsu, complete with ladders, buckets, ropes, brushes, and more than thirty human figures. It is a subject that displays artistry and incredible craftsmanship; it also recalls Japanese tradition, as well as customs both old and new. Sennin, the blind boatman, and characters from various Japanese and Chinese folktales are also favorite Keiun subjects. Many of his designs are most intricate in their execution but have a very "solid" feeling that he thinks is often lacking in antique netsuke. Some of his early netsuke were signed Kogyoku. Hobbies: walking, fishing, reading, and playing *go*.

KENJI 賢次. A.N.: Kenji Abe. Born November 27, 1947, in Tokyo. Studied under Toshikatsu Kobari. Subject: figures of men. Member of J.I.S.A.

KODO 広堂. A.N.: Hiroshi Nakamura. Born September 9, 1923, in Shizuoka Prefecture. F.: Tokutaro. W.: Yoshiko. C.: Satoru. Studied under Kosei. Served in the navy during World War II. Believes action can be better expressed in netsuke than in *okimono*. Subjects from Tokugawa (Edo) period. Member of J.I.S.A.

KOETSU 孝悦. A.N.: Masanosuke Okazaki. Born March 23, 1935, in Tokyo. Descended from a samurai family. F.: Rokunosuke Fujimoto. G.: Tatsuo Okazaki. W.: Sachiko. Learned carving from his father. Material: ivory. Subjects: dragons, flowers, *sennin*, and persimmon with miniature scene inside. Intricate, skillful work. Will be a first-rank carver. Hobbies: oil painting, fishing, and gardening. Member of J.I.S.A. and Chowa-kai.

KOGYOKU (KOGYOKU) (MASATOSHI) (YUJI)   KOKO   KOSEI   KOSEN

KOGYOKU 恍玉. A.N.: Kawashima (given name unknown). All efforts to secure biographical data about this very capable contemporary carver have failed. His netsuke, usually portraying legendary figures, are carved with great skill and imagination. He carves in ivory, giving his netsuke a black-and-white finish and only occasionally using beige tones. He uses four different signatures: Kogyoku 恍玉 on the netsuke he rates as being of top quality, Kogyoku (耕玉 with a different character for *ko*) on his second-quality pieces, Masatoshi 正利 on those ranking third, and Yuji 由次 on those he rates last. The buyer, however, might disagree with Kogyoku's rating of his work.

KOKO 孝子. A.N.: Katsuji Fujimoto. Born September 22, 1925, in Tokyo. F.: Rokunosuke Fujimoto. G.: Kisuke Fujimoto. W.: Teruko. C.: Shuichi, Hidetoshi. Studied under his father, the first Koko (孝古), who was also a carver, as is the younger son, Koetsu (see above). Original designs from Japanese life: children, men with animals, openwork. During the war, carved wooden boxes. Hobbies: painting, attending *waka* (Japanese poetry) meetings, and taking long walks. Member of J.I.S.A.

KOSEI 光声. A.N.: Mitsuo Tamura. Born January 11, 1935, in Ibaraki Prefecture. F.: Katanosuke Tamura. W.: Sachiko. C.: Mika, Yuki. Studied under Hosei. Material: ivory. Subjects: Hotei, men at work, figures from folktales. Hobbies: walking and judo. Member of J.I.S.A. and Chowa-kai.

KOSEN 古仙. A.N.: Masakazu Nagai. Born February 21, 1941, in Chiba Prefecture. F.: Hakusei Nagai (*okimono* carver). G.: Yasunosuke Nagai. Learned to carve from his father, Hakusei. Hobbies: music and keeping small birds. Member of J.I.S.A. and Ushio-kai.

KOYU 弘雄. A.N.: Hiro-o Asai. Born February 13, 1907, in Tokyo. F.: Kanji Asai. G.: Kansai Asai. W.: Terue. C.: Koichi. Studied under his father, Kanji. Material: ivory. Subjects: animals. Member of J.I.S.A. and Aisen-kai.

KOYU
(ASAI)   KOYU
(TANAKA)   MAKOTO   MASATOSHI   MASAYUKI

KOYU 光幽. A.N.: Kazuo Tanaka. Born May 9, 1921, in Fukushima Prefecture. F.: Gisuke Tanaka. W.: Chiyono. C.: Hiroaki, Mieko. Studied under Shiko Hori, whose carving lineage goes back to Tomochika. Was one of five organizers of the J.I.S.A. and is very active in its affairs. Won the Japan Art Association's Appreciation Award at the first Ivory Carving Exhibition. Takes subject matter from old Japanese life and customs, carving mostly realistic figures of men. Best known for his Okubo Hikozaemon (samurai), Noh dancer, old man with flower basket, and old man from China. Very good photogenic composition; careful, skilled, and detailed workmanship; uses stain and color (mostly browns) for design accents. In military service from 1942 to 1946. Hobbies: bowling, traveling, and playing *go*.

MAKOTO 誠. A.N.: Seiichi Aoki. Born July 20, 1934, in Tokyo. F.: Zenshiro Aoki. Material: ivory. Subjects: cormorant fisherman and other subjects from Japanese life. Hobbies: swimming, traveling, and reading. Member of J.I.S.A. and Chowa-kai.

MASATOSHI 雅俊. A.N.: Tokisada Nakamura. Born 1915 in Tokyo. F.: Kuya, a famous carver whose actual name was Takakazu Nakamura. W.: Shizu. C.: one daughter; two grandchildren. Descended from a long line of carvers of Buddhist images. Extremely versatile in style and subject matter. Carves skillfully in both ivory and wood. His imaginative and often humorous designs range from fanciful to realistic animals and birds; from genre to legendary figures; from simple abstractions to intricate, detailed figures. Carves only at night and devotes weeks to his better netsuke. Technical ability unsurpassed in this or any other age. Hobby: photography.

MASAYUKI 政之. A.N.: Katsumasa Nakagawa. Born September 18, 1914, in Tokyo. F.: Monjiro Nakagawa. G.: Isshin Nakagawa. W.: Kimi. C.: Yukio, Aiko. Studied under Hosei. Mostly a finish carver but hopes someday to be a good *issaku* carver. Material: ivory. Subjects: manners and male figures of ancient times. Member of J.I.S.A. and Aisen-kai.

MEIGYOKUSAI (MEIGIN)   MICHITERU   MITSUYUKI   NANRYU

MEIGYOKUSAI 明玉斉. A.N.: Meigin Hiraga. Born 1896 in Tokyo; later moved to Kyoto, where he now resides. F.: Seiki Hiraga. G.: Yoshinosuke Hiraga. W.: Koyoshi. C.: Tanetoshi. Studied under Shogin, whose carving lineage goes back to Gyokuzan. Very versatile in both technique and subject matter. Often draws upon old classical designs for his subjects, but his original designs, like his twelve-animals-of-the-zodiac netsuke, are outstanding. Received prizes for carving before he was twenty-five. Famous not only for his skill as a netsuke carver but also as a *senryu* poet and teacher. His original designs are strong, and pleasing and follow traditional netsuke form. Material: ivory. He rests one day a week and spends the time visiting temples and shrines and attending *senryu* meetings.

MICHITERU 道輝. A.N.: Michiteru Matsuda. Born July 30, 1924 in Tokyo. F.: Hakuraku Matsuda. G.: Naotaro Matsuda. W.: Mitsue. Prefers traditional netsuke subjects, particularly male figures. Material: ivory. Does his own designing and spends an average of twenty days on better netsuke. Hobbies: walking and reading. Member of J.I.S.A. and Aisen-kai.

MITSUYUKI 光行. A.N.: Tsuneo Aoki. Born September 26, 1932, in Ibaraki Prefecture. F.: Genshiro Aoki. G.: Tota Aoki. W.: Sueko. C.: Masahiro, Izumi. Material: ivory. Subjects: Hotei, Noh masks and dancers, and original contemporary designs. Shows great promise. Hobbies: playing *go* and walking. Member of J.I.S.A. and Ushio-kai.

NANRYU 南柳. A.N.: Keizo Kurata. Born October 1935 in Saitama Prefecture. W.: Katsu. C.: Fumihiko, Tomoko. Carving teacher: Sumio Ishida. Very capable and versatile carver. His original designs are drawn from a wide range of Japanese legend and folklore (Fig. 110). Studies hard; very industrious; constantly improving. Name well known among collectors. Hobbies: gardening and swimming. Member of J.I.S.A.

NOBUAKI 信明. A.N.: Nobuichi Hosaka. Born February 6, 1934, in Niigata Prefecture. Subjects: farmers, fishermen. Studied under Kiyo-o Kondo (Seimei).

NOBUAKI   RYOSEI   RYOSEN   RYOSHU   RYOZAN   RYUFU

RYOSEI 梁生. A.N.: Isamu Yabe. Born June 1932 in Saitama Prefecture. F.: Tetsuzo Yabe. Believes that only in netsuke can the real beauty of ivory be shown. Subjects: elegant women of the Edo period. Hobbies: walking and carpentry. Member of J.I.S.A.

RYOSEN 綾泉. A.N.: Masahiro Akita. Born February 17, 1932, in Tokyo. Descended from a samurai family. F.: Tatsugoro Akita. G.: Chokichi Akita. W.: Mitsue. C.: Masakazu. Studied under Binsho Kobari. Belongs to a group of promising young carvers but likes to design netsuke of strong, powerful men like cormorant fishermen and *sennin* rather than innovative abstractions. If he continues to develop, he will be a first-rank carver. Hobby: singing folk songs. Member of J.I.S.A.

RYOSHU 良舟. A.N.: Shozo Miyazawa. Born August 18, 1912, in Tokyo. F.: Seijiro Miyazawa (carving name: Ryoshu). W.: Yaeko. C.: Shotaro, Kiyohiko, Kazuko, Ryoko, Haruko, Kozo, Hideshi, Shimpei. Started to learn carving from his father while in elementary school but devoted most of his time to painting until he went to war. At thirty, returned to civilian life and decided that carving was to be his profession. Known for his *kappa* netsuke. Carves only in ivory. Designs original and carving excellent. In recent years has done considerable experimenting in various design fields, including fish and animal abstractions. Member and former president of J.I.S.A.

RYOZAN 亮山. A.N.: Ryo Okubo. Born November 20, 1913, in Tokyo. Descended from a samurai family. F.: Jirokichi Okubo. G.: Ichizo Okubo. W.: Shizuko. Material: ivory; subjects: old men. Devotes most of his time to carving *okimono*. Member of J.I.S.A. and Aisen-kai.
49
RYUFU 柳風. A.N.: Takeo Fukushima. Born January 1, 1934, in Ibaraki Prefecture. Studied under Sumio Ishida (Seiho). Subject: *sennin*.

RYUHO 龍抱. A.N.: Toshio Komada. Born November 12, 1924, in Tokyo. F.: Fukuichiro Komada (Ryusui). G.: Haruyuki Komada (Ryusai). W.: Sadako. C.:

RYUHO   RYUSHI   SEIDO   SEIGYOKU

Tatsuya, Atsuko. Carving master: Ryusui (his father). Occasionally makes netsuke—elegant ladies—but is best known as an outstanding *okimono* carver. Member of J.I.S.A. and one of its five organizers.

RYUSHI 柳之. A.N.: Isamu Komada. Born February 15, 1934, in Tokyo. F.: Fukuichiro Komada (Ryusui). G.: Haruyuki Komada (Ryusai). W.: Masue. C.: Naoki. Both Ryushi and his brother Ryuho, also an ivory carver, learned carving from their father, Ryusui, whose lineage goes back to Shungetsu, a master carver of the early nineteenth century. Ryushi and Ryuho are nephews of Yoshigoro Komada (Yoko), who was a first-rank netsuke carver. Ryushi started carving at fifteen and has always preferred netsuke carving, since he feels that his particular talent finds its expression in the netsuke art form. Prefers carving figures of women, and his classical Japanese women in both netsuke and small *okimono* have found great favor among collectors. His designs are marked by elegance and sometimes quiet humor; his workmanship is skilled and detailed; and the finish, polish, and coloring of his netsuke are particularly notable. His basic subjects are often found in antique netsuke, but his designs are new and original and are usually figures of men or women exemplifying the manners of the era in history or folklore from which they have been taken. His use of color is pleasing; especially distinctive are his soft rosy-rust shades. He uses only hand tools for carving and polishing and spends at least nine nine-hour days on each netsuke. His netsuke are hand-polished, first with the plant *Equisetum hiemale*, second with sandpaper, and finally with powdered deerhorn. Finds greatest relaxation in traveling. Member of J.I.S.A.

SEIDO 清道. A.N.: Katsuro Ishii. Born October 9, 1934, in Gumma Prefecture. Descended from a samurai family. F.: Kumesaku Ishii. Studied under his brother, Hosei Ishii. One of a group of promising young carvers. Makes imaginative netsuke (girl reading book, god of wind); also makes chessmen and small *okimono*. Hobbies: dancing and bowling. Member of J.I.S.A.

SEIGYOKU 生玉. A.N.: Nobuo Kaneko. Born August 5, 1933, in Tokyo. Descended from the samurai Goemon Kaneko. F.: Sadakichi Kaneko. W.: Michiko. Carving master: Dosei Takeuchi. Skillful carver; his better netsuke of excellent quality.

SEIHO   SEIMEI   SEIRO   SEIRYO   SENPO

Popular with collectors. Original designs from old Japanese legends and folktales. Also talented in painting and poetry. Received Sunamoto award for effort in 1960. Hobbies: gardening, fishing, swimming, and music. Member of J.I.S.A.

SEIHO 声方. A.N.: Katsuro Azuma. Born February 20, 1936, in Ibaraki Prefecture. F.: Kumajiro Azuma. W.: Toshiko. C.: Yasutaka, Noriko, Yuji. Studied with Hosei Meguro. Material: ivory; subjects: usually designs with children—for example, children on a conch shell. Good carver. Hobbies: walking, sports, and reading. Member of J.I.S.A.

SEIMEI 清明. A.N.: Kiyo-o Kondo. Born March 23, 1917, in Tokyo. F.: Fumiaki Kondo. G.: Masaji Kondo (Bummei). W.: Toyo. C.: Akira, Tadashi, Nobuko, Setsuko. Learned to carve from his father. Is a fine *okimono* carver but occasionally carves netsuke. Material: ivory; subjects: figures of women—for example, Fuji Musume and Kiyo (of the Dojo-ji legend). Member of J.I.S.A. (vice-president 1970–71).

SEIRO 青芦. A.N.: Hideo Sumida. Born September 13, 1935, in Kumamoto Prefecture. Descended from a samurai family. F.: Noboru Sumida. G.: Minoshichi Sumida. W.: Haruko. C.: Tomoko. Studied under Seiho Ishida. Does *issaku* netsuke carving as well as finish carving. Likes to do genre figures from ukiyoe sources, but his animals are particularly popular with collectors. Holds promise of being a good carver. Hobbies: swimming, dancing, and skiing. Member of J.I.S.A.

SEIRYO 青涼. A.N.: Jun'ichiro Iwakura. Born November 29, 1939, in Tokyo. F.: Shimmatsu Iwakura. W.: Masa. C.: Atsuko, Eiichi. Studied under Seido Ishida. Material: ivory; subjects: figures of men. Member of J.I.S.A.

SENPO (SEMPO) 仙歩. A.N.: Senkichi Kobayashi. Born March 2, 1919, in Tokyo. Of samurai ancestry. F.: Takeichiro Kobayashi. G.: Matsutaro Shimomura. W.: Michiko. C.: Yuko, Shuichi. Since age sixteen, has been deaf as a result of middle-ear disease. Learned carving from his father, who started to carve netsuke after World War II. Excellent student; is capable of producing exceptionally good netsuke.

SHIKO   SHINGETSU   SHINRYO   SHINSHO

Material: ivory; subjects from history, folktales, and nature. His cicadas are especially noteworthy. Highly skilled at repairing intricate machinery. Hobbies: photography, swimming, traveling, and playing *go*. Member of J.I.S.A.

SHIKO 志光. A.N.: Yasutaro Hori. Born March 1885 in Tokyo; died November 23, 1961. Studied under Masamichi Kuno; teacher of Koyu Tanaka. Versatile in subject matter; subjects include figures of old men, figures of women, and flowers. Vigorous designs taken from everyday life of Edo period.

SHINGETSU 親月. A.N.: Fujio Muramatsu. Born November 18, 1934, in Tokyo. F.: Manjiro Muramatsu (Kogoku), who was an ivory carver and died in 1951. W.: Ryoko. C.: Akiyo, Hiroyuki. Teacher: Shinsho Kikuchi. Material: ivory; subjects: Noh masks and themes from nature. Hobbies: reading and viewing art objects.

SHINRYO 親良. A.N.: Ryozo Suzuki. Born February 27, 1910, in Tokyo. G.: Shigematsu Suzuki (architect). W.: Setsuko. C.: Hiroshi. Studied first under Shunsei Tomioka, famous for his relief carving, and later under Shinsho, one of the leading carvers of the twentieth century. Extremely versatile and imaginative. Has won many prizes, and his work is popular among collectors. Makes interesting realistic netsuke of dogs, tigers, and monkeys as well as highly stylized roosters and hens. Observes many of the old netsuke traditions in form, but his designs are new and fresh. Most of his work has great tactile appeal. Has great feeling for beauty of ivory and brings out its warmth and luster in his creations. Worked in an airplane factory during World War II. Hobbies: gardening and traveling. Member of J.I.S.A. and Aisen-kai.

SHINSHO 親章. A.N.: Yasugoro Kikuchi. Born January 7, 1890, in Tokyo; died March 31, 1971. Carved only ivory. His specialty was figures of people, and he treated his subjects with poetry and elegance. Popular among collectors. Pupil of Komei and exponent of Komei's ideology and style. Was a fine teacher as well as a carver and numbered many well-known contemporary carvers among his pupils, including Shindo, Shingetsu, Shinryo, and Shinzan.

SHINZAN   SHINZAN   SHOBI   SHODO   SHOFU
                 (MASANAO)

SHINZAN 信山. A.N.: Shinkichi Ichikawa. Born January 27, 1948, in Gumma Prefecture. F.: Tomoyoshi Ichikawa. Teacher: Katsuzo Utsuki. Studies hard while doing rough carving; hopes to become an *issaku* carver. Hobbies: swimming, skiing, and listening to recorded music. Member of J.I.S.A.

SHINZAN 辰山 (MASANAO). A.N.: Yoshio Sakai. Born July 11, 1904, in Ise, Mie Prefecture. F.: Seisaburo Sakai, netsuke carver. W.: Takako. C.: Miyo, Setsuko, Hiroko, Eiko. Learned carving from his father, whose professional name was Masakiyo. While in school, showed interest and talent in woodcarving and painting. At eighteen, under his father's tutelage, he began netsuke carving. Carves only in wood: boxwood, olive wood, and a Japanese hardwood called *tochi*. Subjects drawn from classic netsuke designs, mostly from customs, legendary figures, and nature. One of the very few contemporary carvers who work only in wood. Workmanship of highest quality. A sincere person, completely dedicated to the art of netsuke carving.

SHOBI 照美. A.N.: Kintaro Hasegawa. Born November 18, 1906, in Tokyo. F.: Saburo Hasegawa. W.: Shime (deceased). C.: Giichi. Teacher: Shoichiro Hasegawa. Carves in ivory, using old designs and techniques. His netsuke are very round and smooth. Member of J.I.S.A.

SHODO 昇堂. A.N.: Hiroshi Asaoka. Born July 6, 1923, in Tokyo. F.: Otosaburo Asaoka. G.: Hisayoshi Asaoka. W.: Seki. C.: Shiromichi, Teruo. Was a French-cuisine cook after returning from war. Studied under Shomin. Works out designs in detailed sketches drawn from customs and folktales of old Japan and usually includes a man's figure. Master of intricate, detailed carving and quiet, serene designs. Typical subjects: nobleman in a palanquin, Hana-Saka Jijii, two men playing *go* in a pumpkin, Daikoku in a sack. Outstanding ivory carver of the twentieth century. Hobbies: fishing, cultivation of bonsai.

SHOFU 松風. A.N.: Yasuo Amano. Born November 27, 1917, in Chiba Prefecture. F.: Kikuo Amano (Shogetsu). G.: Kisaburo Amano, educator. W.: Shizu. C.: Yukio, Fuku, Hisako. Learned carving from his father, Shogetsu. Carves in ivory.

SHOGEN   SHOGETSU   SHOKO   SHOSAI

Uses the name Shofu when doing *issaku* carving and the name Shozan when doing finish work. Is skilled in reversible-face technique originated by his father. Carves in the style of Shogetsu and may become a first-rate carver. Likes to carve subjects from Noh plays and attends Noh performances when possible. Is skilled in calligraphy, ink painting, and oil painting. Member of Juvenile Welfare Commission. Hobbies: visiting secondhand bookstores and traveling to see old architecture and Buddhist statues. Director of J.I.S.A. and member of Aisen-kai.

SHOGEN 象玄. A.N.: Shuichiro Sato. Born September 24, 1914, in Niigata Prefecture. W.: Mitsue. C.: Shoichi, Miiko, Kensuke, Kuniko. Teacher: Yoshitaro Meguro. Rough carver but occasionally makes netsuke with designs taken from ukiyoe. Member of J.I.S.A.

SHOGETSU 松月. A.N.: Kikuo Amano. Born April 17, 1888, in Tokyo. F.: Kisaburo Amano. W.: Take (d. 1953). C.: Yasuo, Shiro, Goro, Akiyo, Kazuyo. Studied under Shugetsu. Famous for developing the technique of the reversible face. He now carves only netsuke, which are easily recognizable by their elaborately etched decorative patterns and beautiful finish. His subjects are taken from nature and legend, his bonsai devotee being one of his best. Carves only in ivory from original designs. His work is well known and liked by collectors of contemporary netsuke. He is also talented in *yokyoku,* the singing of the Noh drama.

SHOKO 昇己. A.N.: Shotaro Nishino. Born June 26, 1915, in Tokyo; died October 15, 1971. F.: Takizo Nishino. W.: Yasuko. Cousin of the carver Fukujiro Nishino and nephew of the famous Soko Morita. Began to study under Soko at the age of fifteen. Worked almost exclusively in wood. Spent months designing and carving a single netsuke and never repeated a design. Subjects usually drawn from religion and legend but designs always very original and imaginative. Very religious; believed that the soul must be pure before the artist can create a fine work of art. In later years devoted much of his time to carving small Buddhist statues, the most famous being an eight-inch-high image of the Juichimen Senju Kannon done in sandalwood. Most original of the So-school carvers and one of the most skillful and imaginative of

SHUBI   SHUGETSU   SHUHO   SOSUI

twentieth-century carvers. Worked at night, seven nights a week. Had no hobbies. Carving was his life.

SHOSAI 昇斉. A.N.: Toshikazu Saito. Born in Tokyo; died in 1970. Third-generation carver, teacher of his son Bishu, a very promising contemporary carver. Like his son, very imaginative.

SHUBI 秀美. A.N.: Iwao Aramaki. F.: Kazo Aramaki. G.: Munekichi Aramaki. W.: Toshiko. C.: Masako, Reiko. Subject: mainly flowers. Member of J.I.S.A.

SHUGETSU 秀月. A.N.: Junji Arihara. Born March 15, 1918, in Yamagata Prefecture. Carves in ivory—mostly *okimono*, occasionally netsuke. Subjects: Daikoku, Ebisu, Hannya, and other pre-Meiji subjects. Pupil of Buzen Suminishi. Hobbies: playing *shogi* and *go*. Member of J.I.S.A.

SHUHO 珠峯. A.N.: Takeshi Taniguchi. Born August 31, 1933, in Ibaraki Prefecture. Descended from a samurai family. F.: Shozaemon Taniguchi. W.: Hiroko. C.: Junko, Toshikazu, Tsutomu. Self-taught; studies very hard; shows promise of becoming a first-rank carver. Always challenged by the task of bringing designs of his imaginative mind to completed netsuke. Particularly enjoys carving subjects from nature. Hobby: Japanese dancing. Member of J.I.S.A. and chairman of Chowa-kai.

SOSUI 藻水. A.N.: Jiro Ouchi. Born August 5, 1911, in Tokyo; died in November 1972. F.: Jizaemon Ouchi (the famous carver Gyokuso). G.: Asakichi Ouchi. W.: Kiyoko. C.: Kazuko, Tomoko. Began studying under Soko Morita at fifteen. One of the So school's greatest carvers. Had been ill and had not carved since the mid-fifties. Worked mostly in wood, often using combinations of different woods, occasionally in ivory. Very versatile in subjects and techniques. Liked to carve animals, figures from everyday Japanese life, and occasional abstractions. Imaginative designs and meticulous workmanship. His netsuke are eagerly sought by collectors of both antique and contemporary netsuke. Usually spent upwards of a month on each netsuke, working twelve hours a day and seven days a week. His occasional hours of relaxation were

TADAKAZU   TOMOHARU   YASUFUSA   YOKO (KYOKUSEN)

spent in reading, fishing, and calligraphy. During World War II, managed a watch shop and repaired watches. Considered by most authorities as one of the three foremost netsuke carvers of the twentieth century.

TADAKAZU 忠和. A.N.: Kazuo Muroi. Born November 8, 1915, in Tokyo; died October 18, 1974. F.: Chuji Muroi. W.: Hiroko. C.: Toshiyuki. Learned to carve from his father. Did rough carving but occasionally made netsuke. Material: ivory; subject: life of common people in the Edo period. Member of J.I.S.A.

TOMOHARU 友春. A.N.: Gentaro Hamada. Born January 20, 1927, in Tokyo. F.: Shuzan Hamada (netsuke carver). G.: Masaaki Hamada (ivory carver). W.: Kumiko. C.: Kazuo, Miyoko. Teacher: Toshitsugi Kato. Material: ivory, boxwood. Carves *okimono* and occasionally netsuke. Also talented as painter and musician. Member of J.I.S.A.

YASUFUSA 保房. A.N.: Yasuo Saito. Born January 20, 1931, in Tokyo. F.: Yoshiuji Saito. G.: Teruichiro Saito. W.: Yoshiko. C.: two sons. At nineteen, began to learn finish carving under his uncle, Yoshikane, and later, under his father, studied the carving of women's figures. Has been working with his cousin Bishu but has begun to carve *issaku* netsuke. His first netsuke were *manju;* now he carves animals and has exhibited a *shishi,* a rabbit, and a mouse. Shows considerable promise. Hobbies: playing *shogi* and cultivating *bonsai.* Member of J.I.S.A.

YOKO 陽香. A.N.: Yoshigoro Komada. Born December 5, 1885, in Tokyo; died October 31, 1974. F.: Haruyuki Komada (Ryusai), *okimono* carver. G.: Tetsugoro Komada, tailor. Began to learn carving from his father, Ryusai, at age twelve. Material: ivory; subjects taken from Japanese and Chinese life—tranquil, quiet figures. Delicate, detailed composition; skillful and beautiful use of color. Long considered a top-ranking carver and was still alert and carving in his last years. Attended J.I.S.A. meetings and enjoyed contacts with young carvers. Uncle of Ryuho and Ryushi. Used signature Kyokusen 旭泉 on work sold through his agent, Shigeo Tsujita.

YOSHIYUKI   YOSHIYUKI   YUKIMASA (MASATOMO) (TOMOICHI)
(MIYAMOTO)   (SHIBATA)

YOSHIYUKI 芳之. A.N.: Yoshiro Miyamoto. Born June 20, 1916, in Miyagi Prefecture. Studied under his father, Yoshinosuke Miyamoto. Subject: *kozuchi* (small mallet). Member of J.I.S.A.

YOSHIYUKI 芳之. A.N.: Yoshitaro Shibata. Born in 1883 in Tokyo; died of a heart attack on December 27, 1970, while carving a netsuke. Descended from a samurai family. F.: Kenjiro Shibata. W.: Hatsuko. Brother was a Noh actor. Cousins: Kanzan Shimomura, painter; Kiyotoki Shimomura, carver of Noh masks. Studied under Kanzan Shimomura with the idea of becoming a painter but, during his twenties, became very much interested in netsuke carving and began to study under Nobuyoshi Suzuki, a noted carver of the Tomochika school. Best known for his monkey-mimic, Oharame (flower vendor of Ohara), *masuotoshi, oni,* and *rakan* netsuke. Very faithful to old netsuke tradition in feeling. Great attention to detail; original, amusing designs. Used incense smoke instead of stain to achieve a soft tint in ivory. Sometimes used semiprecious-stone inlay and color for decoration. Generally considered a first-rate carver. Hobby: fishing.

YUKIMASA 幸正. A.N.: Tadami Uno. Born in November 1914 in Gifu City, where he still lives. F.: Shintaro Uno (architect). W.: Harue. C.: Kotaro. Studied under Koshin Akiyama, who carved netsuke, *okimono,* and Buddha statues in both ivory and wood and whose father was a famous carver of fans. Has been carving since 1930 and concentrates on netsuke for the foreign collectors' market. Some eighty to ninety percent of his netsuke are exported. Especially known for his original designs portraying life and customs of the Edo period and for his animals. Usually uses ivory but occasionally boxwood. Sometimes uses stain, color, or inlay. Originally wanted to be a painter; has exhibited and won prizes with his photographs. For four years during the war, stopped carving and made models of airplanes. His wife assists him by doing all staining, coloring, and polishing. Uses the name Yukimasa 幸正 on good works, Masatomo 正友 on works of medium quality, and Tomoichi 友一 on animals. Hobbies: photography, fishing, writing poetry, listening to classical and popular music.

YUKO 友光. A.N.: Toshitake Nakamura. Born February 21, 1916, in Saitama

YUKO   (SOMEI)

Prefecture. F.: Kiyosaku Nakamura. G.: Yozaemon Nakamura. W.: Sumiko. C.: Shuichi, Toshihiko. Uses name Somei 宗明 on his *okimono*. Uses both ivory and wood (boxwood, sandalwood, cherry) in carving netsuke; also combinations of ivory and wood. Makes carved-nut netsuke as well. Subjects include figures of men in Japanese life and religion. Is especially well known for animal and insect netsuke. Hobbies: gardening, swimming, movies, and baseball. Member of J.I.S.A., in which he has been very active since its formation, and of Aisen-kai.

List of Contemporary Okimono Carvers

AKIRA   BINSHO   HIROYUKI   HOGETSU   JOGYOKU

KEY TO ABBREVIATIONS

A.N.: actual name   W.: wife's name
F.   father's name   C.: names of children
G.: grandfather's name

AKIRA 章. A.N.: Akira Suzuki. Born July 14, 1945, in Ibaraki Prefecture. Studied under Hakusei Nagai. Subject: figures of men. Member of J.I.S.A.

BINSHO 敏生. A.N.: Toshikatsu Kobari. Born March 14, 1925, in Tochigi Prefecture. F.: Tokichi Kobari. G.: Tosaku Kobari. W.: Chiyoko. C.: Naoki, Hiromi.

HIROYUKI 広之. A.N.: Minoru Sakurai. Born January 26, 1930, in Tokyo. Studied under his father, Kosei Sakurai.

HOGETSU 峰月. A.N.: Shimpei Ishiwatari. Born November 11, 1921, in Ibaraki Prefecture. Studied under Seishu Suzuki. Subject: dragons.

JOGYOKU 如玉. A.N.: Tsutomu Narita. Born January 23, 1944, in Tokyo. Studied under the first-generation carver Jogyoku Narita. Subject: basket makers. Member of J.I.S.A.

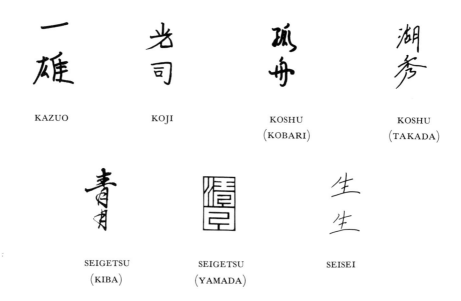

KAZUO 一雄. A.N.: Kazuo Tsukada. Born December 14, 1915, in Tokyo. Studied under Tokichi Tsukada. Subject: animals. Member of J.I.S.A.

KOJI 光司. A.N.: Kiyoshi Yamaai. Born July 20, 1932, in Yamaguchi Prefecture. F.: Morio Yamaai. W.: Ai. C.: Takashi, Wakako. Studied under Komin Matsuno. Material: ivory. Creates his own designs, usually of birds. Member of J.I.S.A. and Chowa-kai.

KOSHU 孤舟. A.N.: Michiaki Kobari. Born in Tochigi Prefecture (date unknown). F.: Tokichi Kobari. G.: Tosaku Kobari. Member of J.I.S.A.

KOSHU 湖秀. A.N.: Uichi Takada. Born August 29, 1903, in Tokyo. Studied under Kanko Harada. Subject: flowers. Member of J.I.S.A.

SEIGETSU 青月 (RYUGETSU 柳月). A.N.: Yoshio Kiba. Born September 17, 1935, in Saitama Prefecture.

SEIGETSU 清月. A.N.: Akira Yamada. Born August 12, 1944, in Saitama Prefecture. Studied under Kaneharu Yamada. Subjects: Ebisu and Daikoku. Member of J.I.S.A.

SEISEI 生生. A.N.: Takeuchi (given name unknown). Born April 16, 1921, in Himeji; died March 1966. Studied under Ryusui Komada. Very good carver of traditional netsuke subjects.

SHINSEI   SHINZAN   SHUGETSU   SHUHO

SHUNSUI   TAKAMITSU   YAMAJI   YOZAN

SHINSEI 信生. A.N.: Nobuo Shimizu. Born August 21, 1944, in Saitama Prefecture. Studied under Toshikatsu Kobari. Subject: figures of men. Member of J.I.S.A.

SHINZAN 親山. A.N.: Toshio Shimura. Born January 20, 1931, in Yamanashi Prefecture. Studied under Shisho Kikuchi. Subject: classical customs. Member of J.I.S.A.

SHUGETSU 秀月. A.N.: Sachinori Watanabe. Born May 4, 1915, in Gifu Prefecture. Studied under Kaneharu Yamada. Subject: mainly figures of men. Member of J.I.S.A.

SHUHO 秀方. A.N.: Michio Yagawa. Born June 18, 1919, in Tokyo. Studied under Koshu Takada. Subject: roses. Member of J.I.S.A.

SHUNSUI 春水. A.N.: Toshiaki Kobari. Born January 28, 1923, in Tokyo. Studied under his brother, Toshikatsu Kobari. Subject: figures of men. Member of J.I.S.A.
20
TAKAMITSU 孝光. A.N.: Bunji Yokota. Born December 2, 1901, in Tokyo. Member of J.I.S.A.

YAMAJI 山路. A.N.: Mitsuharu Yamaji. Born April 21, 1901, in Tokyo. Subjects: pheasants, golden pheasants, owls, peacocks, and other birds.

YOZAN 陽山. A.N.: Takeji Onizawa. Born December 23, 1899, in Chiba Prefecture. Studied under Chikamasa Tomioka. Member of J.I.S.A.

The Japan Ivory Sculptors' Association

The art of netsuke carving, dormant during the artistically lifeless Meiji era (1868–1912), was affected by several factors:

1. The decline in the use and popularity of netsuke in Japan
2. The export of antique netsuke to the foreign collectors' market
3. The attempt by some carvers to "cash in" on this newfound market by making quick, cheap copies for export
4. The preference for ivory in the export market and the resultant development in the skill of carving in this medium

Despite the bad image that poor, cheap exports were giving to modern netsuke, the artist-carvers were continuing to pass their skill on to young carvers. But the traditional method of training artists through the master-apprenticeship relationship was rapidly disappearing. In 1876, an art school was established at Kobu University, in the Tokyo area. In 1887, the Tokyo Art Academy was established by legislation, and the first professor of the sculpture department was a netsuke carver, as were several other faculty members, including the famous Gyokuzan. The student-artist was learning the history of art, the methods of ancient carving, and allied subjects through modern educational methods. Netsuke carvers still took instruction from master carvers, but their work began to show a fresh, independent, and creative approach rather than the characteristic style and technique of the professional schools of the various masters to whom the earlier carvers were apprenticed.

With the support of twenty or more dealers in ivory carvings, the Tokyo Carvers' Association was formed in 1877. It included Kaneda, Gyokuzan, Mitsuaki, and other well-known carvers as charter members. Originally, the members met each month at Kaneda's home. During the next ten years, the membership grew, and the organization's name and meeting place changed several times. In 1887, the original name was restored, and monthly meetings featuring lectures by outstanding members of the art community were established. An annual carving contest was inaugurated, and study meetings were held at the Seibikan, a showroom where a continual display of carvings by members could be viewed. The Imperial Household gave encouragement to the association and occasionally favored it with orders. The end of this fine organization came when it merged with the Japan Art Association in 1924, a year after the Seibikan was destroyed in the Great Kanto Earthquake.

Early in the twentieth century, several smaller groups were formed. They included the Kogi-kai, for carvers of high skill; the Hakucho-kai, for division (*bungyo*) workers in ivory; the Aicho-kai, organized by young ivory carvers after their return from service in World War II; and the Shinsen-kai, for teacher-class and elder carvers. These early groups were very exclusive and usually confined their membership to those belonging to a certain "school" of carvers.

In 1964, five young carvers, each belonging to a different group—Koyu Tanaka, Binsho Kobari, Ichio Sakurai, Hozan Fujita, and Ryuho Komada—started to organize a new association in the belief and hope that much could be learned from an exchange of ideas and techniques regardless of age and school. Through their efforts, the Shinsen-kai, the Hakucho-kai, and the Ushio-kai merged and formed the nucleus of the Japan Ivory Sculptors' Association. Of approximately 150 ivory carvers in Japan today, roughly 120 live in or near Tokyo, and 100 of this number, including most of the first-rank netsuke carvers, belong to the J.I.S.A. Of the total number of ivory carvers in Japan today, not more than twenty percent or so would qualify as complete-work (*issaku*) netsuke carvers.

The main purpose of this association is an exchange of ideas—new tools, techniques, materials, designs—any ideas for the improvement of the carver's skill. A secondary purpose of the group is the social aspect, the forming of friendships among men of mutual interests and talents. Meetings are held bimonthly, usually in a room at the City Hall in Kita-ku, Tokyo. Once a year, the carvers have an exhibition of their work for study and discussion. The association has an insurance plan with death benefits for members and a fund from which they help members when they are ill, if help is needed.

Within the J.I.S.A. are two groups that usually meet and display new work once between the bimonthly meetings of the main organization. These two groups are the Chowa-kai, consisting of the young carvers between twenty and forty years of age, and the Aisen-kai, consisting of the carvers who are forty and over. There are six members of the young group who are only twenty years old, but the average age of the Chowa-kai membership is close to thirty-five.

The J.I.S.A. has not allied itself with any general art society. Its members believe that international influence is creeping into other art forms through such art societies, and artist-carvers feel strongly that their art should be preserved essentially in the traditional form and with a distinct Japanese character.

From time to time, questionnaires are submitted to the J.I.S.A. membership, which includes division workers as well as netsuke and *okimono* artist-carvers. The answers bring interesting facts and trends to the surface. For example, at their summer meeting in 1970, fifty-seven members answered a questionnaire similar to one submitted in 1969. A review of some of the answers is revealing.

To the question "Is your father an ivory carver?" forty percent answered "Yes" and fifty-three percent answered "No." The remaining seven percent gave no answer.

Another question was "Do you intend for your child to be an ivory carver?" The answers here are interesting in comparison with those of the 1969 questionnaire: "Yes" for only thirteen percent in 1969 but for twenty-three percent in 1970; "No" for fifty-eight percent in 1969 and for fifty-four percent in 1970. In 1969, nine percent indicated that the decision would be up to the child, while twenty percent gave no answer. In 1970, fourteen percent gave the answer "Already carving," and nine percent gave no answer.

In the 1970 questionnaire, the query "To what group do you belong?" elicited the information that twenty-one did rough carving (*arabori*), fifteen did finishing work (*shiage*), and nineteen did complete work (*issaku*). Two of the members gave no reply.

The age distribution, as indicated by responses to the 1970 questionnaire, was as follows:

Age	Rough Carver	Finisher	Complete Worker
Under 30	4	1	1
31 to 40	8	3	1
41 to 50	1	4	4
51 to 60	5	4	6
Over 60	3	3	7

Although these answers came from only slightly more than half of the J.I.S.A. membership, they seem to indicate a lessening of interest among the young in the art or profession of ivory carving, despite an apparent increase in the number of fathers who want their sons to become carvers.

The question regarding the number of hours worked per day brought forth the following information:

Hours	1969	1970
8	3%	36%
10	37%	50%
12	22%	5%
14	11%	2%

Although twenty-seven percent of the carvers gave no answer in 1969 and seven percent gave no answer in 1970, these figures indicate a trend away from the sunrise-
to-sunset day once observed by most carvers. Also, according to the questionnaire,
the majority of contemporary carvers take off one day per week, whereas it is said
the carvers of early times rarely remained away from their carving more than one
day per month.

It is often asked how much money an ivory carver makes today. His income will
fluctuate, particularly if he is an artist-carver, but according to a 1970 questionnaire
filled out by about sixty percent of the J.I.S.A. membership, the majority of division
workers at that time made roughly $225 to $300 per month. The *issaku* carver made
from $140 to $300. Since that time, the income of the carvers, particularly the first-
rank *issaku* carvers, has increased materially. In 1972, one of Japan's largest dealers
said he had raised his rate of payment to his first-rank carvers twenty percent each
year and that they were currently averaging 150,000 yen per month. At the rate of
exchange at that time, this was close to $500. This amount would have been a fortune
to the netsuke carver of the eighteenth or nineteenth century, or even the first half of
the twentieth century. Today, however, with the tremendous escalation in living costs,
the carver's basic needs, to say nothing of the cost of educating his children, make
demands that pose serious income-versus-outgo problems. The carver loves his work
and the creative outlet it provides for his talent. But how long will he be able to
afford this life and the integrity represented by time-consuming perfection in his
work?

To visit a J.I.S.A. meeting, an outsider would assume these problems are not yet
crucial. The enthusiasm of the members, their interest in any matters pertaining to
their profession, their obvious pleasure in seeing and greeting their peers and elders,
seem to assure the continuance of Japan's traditional netsuke art by a group, albeit
small, of talented, skilled artists.

THE J.I.S.A. EXHIBITION

Before we left for Japan in late October 1971, word came to us through Mr. Nakamura, the J.I.S.A. secretary, that the netsuke carvers in the association wanted to
give an exhibition in our honor during our stay in Tokyo. We were excited over the
invitation, for it meant that we would meet many carvers as well as see netsuke
designs never previously shown.

On November 5, we were driven to the Emmei-in, a temple in Taito Ward. At the
entrance, we were welcomed by the J.I.S.A. officers, and our attention was called to
a stone monument, the only memorial to Japan's netsuke artists. The names of many
of the great carvers have been inscribed on it, and new names are still being added.

159. J.I.S.A. exhibition.

After walking through the beautiful garden, we entered a large room where fifty or sixty carvers had already gathered. More than forty had one or more netsuke on exhibit. They were displayed on low tea tables, and each carver stood in front of his own work. Michi Matsumoto walked along with us, doing simultaneous interpretation and enabling us to visit with each carver and discuss his work with him.

It was a thrilling experience for us, and in spite of the language barrier we could sense the carvers' excitement and pleasure. The day before, my husband and I had appeared on national Japanese television in a program comparable to NBC's "Today" show. We discussed netsuke collecting among foreigners, with particular emphasis on contemporary netsuke and the living carvers. A film clip of Ichiro at work had preceded our interview. It was the first time a program on netsuke had appeared on TV in Japan, and it caused great excitement among the carvers, most of whom had watched it. They also expressed great enthusiasm over my plans for this book, and, most of all, they were interested in us as collectors. These carvers spend

their entire creative working lives on netsuke that are purchased by foreigners whom they don't know and whose interest in netsuke is a great source of puzzlement to them. We were the first collectors most of them had ever met, and they bombarded us with questions for over an hour. They wanted to know why and when we started to collect netsuke, what subjects and carving styles interested us, whether we insisted on functional qualities, how we displayed our netsuke, and many other things.

The opportunity to associate the face and personality of the carver with his work was a privilege few netsuke collectors are able to enjoy. The netsuke exhibited that day ranged from mediocre to excellent, with some innovative designs that were truly exciting. Although the quality of workmanship and design varied, a common denominator was evident in the room. Here was a large group of talented, skilled men—old and young—who were dedicated to their profession and enthusiastic about it but who also realized that they must produce work of high quality in order to command the prices necessary to provide a living in Japan's highly inflated economy.

Speeches by the officers and my husband followed our tour of the exhibit. We were then served sakè and elaborate refreshments, and the serious, almost formal, atmosphere soon became very social and gay. From the Emmei-in we were taken through the beautiful Rikugien garden to a hall, often used by the carvers, where we met with the J.I.S.A. committee appointed to assist me with my book. A nearby room soon filled with most of the rest of the carvers who had been at the exhibit. They repeatedly sent one of their group into our meeting asking us to join them, but the chairman of the committee was very businesslike and insisted upon continuing our session, which was mutually interesting and informative. We finally had to leave because Ichiro's daughter was waiting to serve us dinner. Had we adjourned to the other room, it would have been quite a night. Some of the carvers didn't get home until dawn the next morning.

The new dimension in our netsuke collecting—contact with the carvers—was adding more and more pleasure not only to our collecting itself but also to our life.

List of Netsuke Dealers

Japan

TOKYO

ASAHI ART COMPANY. 3-10, 4-chome, Jingumae, Shibuya-ku. Telephone: 408-4624. G. Fujishiro, president. High-quality antique art objects including occasional good contemporary netsuke. Mrs. Wakayama is very helpful.

HAKUSUI IVORY COMPANY, LIMITED. Shops located in Hotel New Japan, Hotel New Otani, and Hotel Okura. Owned by the Watanabe family, which has a fine and longstanding reputation in the retailing of ivory carvings. Shops carry netsuke in wide price range, including many by first-rank artists.

HODOTA IVORY. Imperial Hotel arcade. K. Hodota, president. Dealers in ivory carvings and accessories since 1890. Wide assortment of contemporary netsuke, including pieces by many first-rank carvers.

K. ITOH. 28, Kamiya-cho, Shiba, Minato-ku. Very dependable dealer with fairly large stock of netsuke, mostly antique.

MIYAKOSHI SHOJI K.K. Palace Hotel Arcade. T. Miyakoshi, president. Specializes in ivory and tortoise-shell work. Wide assortment of netsuke, including pieces by many first-rank artists.

OHNO ART COMPANY. 31-23, 2-chome, Yushima, Bunkyo-ku. Telephone: 811-4365. Y. Ohno, president. One of To-kyo's fine antique-art stores, carrying many beautiful antique netsuke and *inro*. Also a few contemporary netsuke of good quality.

SUNAMOTO IVORY AND COMPANY, LIMITED. 14, 1-chome, Yuraku-cho, Chiyo-da-ku. (Across from Imperial Hotel Annex.) Telephone: 591–5610. S. Suna-moto, president. Has large stock of first-quality contemporary netsuke as well as many in lower price range. Mr. Sunamoto has done much to encourage and promote contemporary carvers. His assistant, Mrs. Kawashima, is very helpful.

TAKASHIMAYA DEPARTMENT STORE. Nihombashi, Chuo-ku. Netsuke varying in age, price, and quality can be found in the antique department in the second basement.

TORAYA ART COMPANY. 13-1, 5-chome, Minami Aoyama, Minato-ku. Usually has a sizable stock of netsuke, both antique and contemporary, ranging from very good to mediocre in quality.

YAMATO BROTHERS. 12-12, 6-chome, Ginza, Chuo-ku. Telephone: 571-2688. H. Nakayama, owner. Carries contemporary netsuke of first quality as well as some of medium grade. Very helpful to novice and knowledgeable collector alike. Mr. Nakayama, like his now deceased father, has long been known as a reliable ivory dealer.

245

KYOTO

KENZO IMAI. 200 Shimmonzen Street. Very knowledgeable antique-netsuke dealer. Handles very few contemporary netsuke, but these are always of good quality.

S. SAWAMURA. Kawara-machi, Oike Minami. Nice person, interesting shop, and occasionally a few good netsuke.

Y. TSURUKI. Higashi-oji. Very well-known dealer who usually has a few excellent contemporary pieces among his stock of antique netsuke.

YAGI ART SHOP. 200 Shimmonzen Street. Good netsuke, mostly of the antique kind, usually sold here.

YOKOYAMA, INCORPORATED. Nawate, Higashiyama-ku. K. Yokoyama, president. Excellent contemporary and antique netsuke can be found among the rather large stock of this store. Mr. Yokoyama, now in his eighties, is interesting and knowledgeable.

Note: There are contemporary netsuke of all qualities to be found in various Kyoto hotel arcades and at the Kyoto Handicraft Center.

YOKOHAMA

S. KANEKO. 8, 1-chome, Honcho, Naka-ku. Telephone: 201-3229. Mr. Kaneko is a well-known and long-respected dealer who often has both contemporary and antique netsuke of very high quality.

MIYANOSHITA

EDO AND COMPANY. T. Inoue, president. Contemporary netsuke of first quality can usually be bought from Mr. Inoue, a reliable and interesting person.

United States

NEW YORK CITY

CHARLES AND COMPANY, IMPORTS, INCORPORATED. The Plaza Hotel, Fifth Avenue at 59th Street. Sizable stock of contemporary netsuke, mostly middle range in price and quality.

FELICE FEDDER, INCORPORATED. 415 East 53rd Street.

HARTMAN GALLERIES. 978 Madison Avenue. Large stock of netsuke, including many of good or fine quality.

IKARI. 45 West 8th Street.

JOSEPH U. SEO. 756 Madison Avenue. Usually has stock of excellent netsuke.

BOSTON

H. YATSUHASHI. 420 Boylston Street. Carries high-grade netsuke, with occasional fine contemporary pieces.

DEEP RIVER, CONNECTICUT

RARE ORIENTAL ARTS. 71 Middlesex Pike. Betty and Walter Killam, owners. First-quality contemporary netsuke are frequently on sale, as well as good to excellent antique netsuke. Mrs. Killam is interested and active in the netsuke field.

WASHINGTON, D.C.

SIMON KRIEGER, INCORPORATED. 712 12th Street, N.W. For many years has carried netsuke of all kinds, good to excellent in quality and covering a wide range of prices.

CHARLESTON, S. CAROLINA

RED TORII ANTIQUES. 197 King Street. Rose and Dan Bowman, owners. Large stock of netsuke, including a sizable percentage of contemporary netsuke, many of which are by first-rank carvers.

CHICAGO

H. NAGATANI. 848 North Michigan Avenue.

SEATTLE

FOX'S JADE SHOP. 1318 Fifth Avenue. Estate collections of good netsuke, mostly antique, are frequently sold in this shop.

OCEANIC TRADING COMPANY. 84 University Street. Herman Krupp, owner. Mr. Krupp has been an importer of Japanese art objects, particularly netsuke, since before World War II. He is most helpful to novice collectors, and many of our best contemporary netsuke were purchased from him.

SANKY'S. 1335 Fourth Avenue. Occasionally, good to excellent contemporary netsuke can be found here.

SAN FRANCISCO

ASHKENAZIE AND CO. Fairmont Hotel, 950 Mason Street. Jade and Oriental art. Best stock of first-quality netsuke in San Francisco. Also excellent antique netsuke. Mr. Askenazie is knowledgeable, helpful, and genuinely interested in netsuke art.

THE DAIBUTSU. 3028 Fillmore Street. Ichiro Shibata, manager.

FOX'S ST. FRANCIS. St. Francis Hotel. William Wright, manager.

G. T. MARSH AND COMPANY. 522 Sutter Street. High-quality Oriental art objects, including netsuke, with some pieces by top-ranking contemporary artists.

T. Z. SHIOTA. 3131 Fillmore Street.

LOS ANGELES

WILLIAM GRISWOLD. 560 South Fair Oaks Avenue, Pasadena.

SETAY GALLERY. Beverly Hills.

HUBERT WEISER. 3749 Shannon Road. Knowledgeable collector of Oriental art objects who is familiar with all antique stores in Los Angeles area and buys both antique and contemporary netsuke from various dealers for resale to clients.

Note: Large department stores, including Bullock's Wilshire and Ohrbach's, occasionally have good contemporary netsuke for sale in their jewelry departments. Most of the large hotels have Oriental art shops that carry netsuke. Contemporary netsuke of mediocre quality, as well as occasional good pieces, are found in Little Tokyo shops in downtown Los Angeles, in Chinatown shops, in the Farmers' Market, and in other shopping centers featuring imports.

LAGUNA BEACH, CALIFORNIA

WARREN IMPORTS. Harry Lawrence, owner. Has a large stock of excellent Oriental art objects, both antique and contemporary, and is increasing its stock of contemporary netsuke.

LAHAINA, MAUI, HAWAII

THE GALLERY. Tim Morrow, owner; Walter G. Kreiner, curator. Specializes in Oriental porcelains, jade, and netsuke. Has large stock of netsuke, half of which are contemporary and include some pieces by first-rank carvers.

KAHALUU, OAHU

ANTIQUES AND JUNQUE. 47–659 Kamehameha Highway.

HONOLULU, OAHU

FAR EAST ANTIQUITIES. Hilton Hawaiian Village shopping area. Mrs. Sharon Beck, owner. Carries good-quality netsuke, among which are some by first-rank contemporary carvers. Mrs. Beck is helpful and reliable.

ORIENTAL TREASURES AND POINTS WEST. Proprietor: Bernard Hurtig. P. O. Box 10698, Honolulu, Hawaii 96816. Tel. (808) 373–9240. Probably the world's largest available stock of first-quality antique and contemporary netsuke. By appointment only.

Note: Netsuke of varying quality can be found at arcade shops in the Royal Hawaiian and other hotels on Waikiki Beach, in Kilohana and other shopping squares, at the Ala Moana shopping center, and in various shops throughout the city that carry Oriental imports.

Canada
TORONTO

REAL AND RARE GALLERY, LIMITED. 1430 Yonge Street.

Europe
LONDON

W. BARRETT AND SON. 9 Old Bond Street. Knowledgeable dealer carrying good to excellent netsuke, including occasional first-quality contemporary pieces.

JOHN CRICHTON. 34 Brook Street. Source for many netsuke collectors.

J. E. ESKENAZI. 166 Piccadilly, Foxglove House. One of the leading buyers of quality netsuke at London auctions.

S. MARCHANT AND SON. 120 Kensington Church Street. Good source of first-quality netsuke, mostly antique.

GEOFFREY MOSS. 51 Brook Street. Source for many netsuke collectors.

SPINK AND SONS. 567 King Street, St. James.

DOUGLAS WRIGHT. 34 Curzon Street. Frequently has excellent netsuke including some contemporary pieces, and often buys for clients at London auctions. A very knowledgeable and helpful dealer specializing in Oriental art.

PARIS

S. AOYAMA. 11 Quai St.-Michel.

G. CRUTEL. 146 Boulevard Haussmann.

SOUSTIEL. 39 Rue de Constantinople.

BRUSSELS

ALAIN TOMMENNE GALLERY. Grand Sablon.

MAISON L. MICHIELS. 34 Rue de la Régence.

ROME

ASIA ARTS. Lungotevere Flamingo, 14 A.

CARIJO. Via del Corso, 157.

MILAN

ESKENAZI. 15 Via Monte Napoleon.

COPENHAGEN

KINCH AND CHRISTENSEN. Ostergrade 16, 1100 Kobenhavn K.

Bibliography

Boger, H. Batterson: *The Traditional Arts of Japan*. Doubleday, Garden City, New York, 1964. Wide range of information on Japan's traditional arts, including netsuke.

Brockhaus, Albert: *Netsuke*, translated by M. R. Watty. Duffield, 1924; reprinted by Hecker Art Books, New York, 1969. The original, from which this greatly abridged version was taken, was published in German in 1905. It was the first serious book on the subject, and it is still considered a netsuke bible by collectors.

Bushell, Raymond: *Collectors' Netsuke*. Weatherhill, New York and Tokyo, 1971. A very informative and interesting study for the sophisticated collector; deals with many early carvers and their netsuke; all photographs in color.

_____: *Netsuke Familiar and Unfamiliar: New Principles for Collecting*. Weatherhill, New York and Tokyo, 1975. An excellent and thoroughly reliable guide for the collector in an age of steadily rising prices; all netsuke photographs in color.

_____: *The Netsuke Handbook of Ueda Reikichi*. Tuttle, Tokyo and Rutland, Vermont, 1961. One of the most useful netsuke books published to date; especially helpful for its listing of carvers and their signatures.

_____: *The Wonderful World of Netsuke*. Tuttle, Tokyo and Rutland, Vermont, 1964. Has limited text but more than 100 photographs of excellent netsuke with informative captions.

Cammann, Schuyler: *Substance and Symbol in Chinese Toggles*. University of Pennsylvania Press, 1959; Oxford University Press, 1962. A scholarly treatise on the Chinese counterpart of netsuke.

Chiba, Reiko: *The Japanese Fortune Calendar*. Tuttle, Tokyo and Rutland, Vermont, 1965. An interesting little book on the twelve animals frequently found in netsuke art.

_____: *The Seven Lucky Gods of Japan*. Tuttle, Tokyo and Rutland, Vermont, 1966. An informative companion to the fortune-calender book, on gods who often appear as netsuke subjects.

Davey, Neil K.: *Netsuke*. Faber & Faber, London, 1974, in association with Sotheby, Parke Bernet Publications. A study based on the M. T. Hindson collection.

Davis, F. Hedland: *Myths and Legends of Japan*. Harrop, London, 1912.

Dorson, Richard M.: *Folk Legends of Japan*. Tuttle, Tokyo and Rutland, Vermont, 1962.

249

Edmunds, Will H.: *Pointers and Clues to the Subjects of Chinese and Japanese Art.* Sampson Low, Marston, London, 1934.

Gorham, Hazel H.: *Japanese Netsuke.* Yamagata Printing Company, Yokohama, 1957. A brief but pleasing volume by an Englishwoman who also wrote on Japanese and other Oriental pottery, Japanese flower arrangement, tray gardens, and kindred subjects.

Griffin, William Elliott: "Japanese Ivory Carvings." *Harper's New Monthly Magazine,* April 1888. Probably the earliest magazine article on netsuke published in the United States.

Halford, Aubrey S. and Giovanna M.: *The Kabuki Handbook.* Tuttle, Tokyo and Rutland, Vermont, 1956. Helpful in identifying Kabuki characters often found in netsuke art.

Hearn, Lafcadio: *Japan: An Attempt at Interpretation.* Tuttle, Tokyo and Rutland, Vermont, 1955. Reprint of a classic introduction to Japanese culture, originally published in 1904.

Hurtig, Bernard, compiler: *Masterpieces of Netsuke Art: One Thousand Favorites of Leading Collectors.* Weatherhill, New York and Tokyo, 1973 (published for the International Netsuke Collectors' Society). Superlative netsuke from twenty leading collections, all shown in full color and actual size.

Jahss, Melvin and Betty: *Inro and Other Miniature Forms of Japanese Lacquer Art.* Tuttle, Tokyo and Rutland, Vermont, 1971. Emphasizes lacquerwork but contains an interesting chapter titled "The Netsuke as an Art Form."

Joly, Henri L.: *Legend in Japanese Art.* Tuttle, Tokyo and Rutland, Vermont, 1967. Fascimile reprint of a very detailed account of legendary subject matter found in all Japanese art, including netsuke. Originally published in 1908.

Jonas, F. M.: *Netsuke.* Kegan Paul, Trench, Trubman, London, 1928; reprinted by Tuttle, Tokyo and Rutland, Vermont, 1960. First book (and for a long time the only available book) on netsuke in English; method of listing signatures in appendix is very helpful to advanced collectors.

Lazarnick, George: *The Signature Book of Netsuke, Inro and Ojime Artists in Photographs.* Reed Publishers, Honolulu, 1976. Comprehensively covers an area of prime importance to discriminating collectors. Almost 1,500 photographs of signatures, 335 of subjects, and 2,063 of individual characters employed in signatures.

Meinertzhagen, Frederick: *The Art of the Netsuke Carver.* Routledge and Kegan Paul, London, 1956. Good for advanced collectors; only book on netsuke containing lineage charts of important carvers.

Michener, James A.: *The Hokusai Sketchbooks.* Tuttle, Tokyo and Rutland, Vermont, 1958. Great source of subject ideas for carvers, many of whom owned copies of Hokusai's sketchbooks.

Newman, Alex R., and Ryerson, Egerton: *Japanese Art: A Collector's Guide.* G. Bell and Sons, London, 1964; reprinted by A. S. Barnes, South Brunswick, New Jersey, 1966. Covers a broad field, with considerable valuable information on netsuke.

Noma, Seiroku: *Masks,* with English adaptation by Meredith Weatherby. Tuttle, Tokyo and Rutland, Vermont, 1957. This small volume includes material on masks used as motifs in both contemporary and ancient netsuke.

O'Brien, Mary Louise: *Netsuke: A Guide for Collectors.* Tuttle, Tokyo and Rutland, Vermont, 1965. One of the recent books on netsuke; a useful guide for beginning collectors.

Okada, Yuzuru: *Netsuke: A Miniature Art of Japan.* Japan Travel Bureau, Tokyo, 1962. Excellent for beginners; section on facsimile signatures also valuable to sophisticated collectors.

Roth, Stig: *Netsuke in the Collections of the Rohss Museum of Arts and Crafts, Goteborg.* Wasatryckeriet, 1970. Particularly interesting for photographs of this famous collection.

Ryerson, Egerton: *The Netsuke of Japan.* G. Bell and Sons, London, 1958; reprinted by A. S. Barnes, Cranbury, New Jersey, 1958. Best book available for beginners on netsuke subject matter.

Sakade, Florence: *Japanese Children's Favorite Stories.* Tuttle, Tokyo and Rutland, Vermont, 1953. Favorite fairy tales, delightfully illustrated with motifs often found in netsuke art.

Sakai, Atsuharu: *Japan in a Nutshell.* Yamagata Printing Company, Yokohama, vol. 1, 1949; vol. 2, 1952. Customs and costumes, as well as folktales and historical, religious, and legendary figures are found in this potpourri of Japanese information.

Volker, T.: *The Animal in Far Eastern Art, Especially in the Art of the Japanese Netsuke.* E. J. Brill, Leyden, 1950. Unsurpassed for treatment of animals in netsuke.

Yasuda, Yuri: *Old Tales of Japan.* Second ed., Tuttle, Tokyo and Rutland, Vermont, 1953. Contains much favorite netsuke story material.

Glossary-Index

Note: Page references precede figure references, and the latter, in general, are to both illustrations and captions. The word "carver" alone designates a netsuke carver, while carvers of *okimono* are specifically designated as such.